Praise

'Zareen's story is inspiring and enlightening. She has faced tragedy and risen above it. She has created a business that positively impacts everyone it touches. She leads with grace, femininity and determination. In every way, Zareen is someone who I find to be an ideal mentor and example of what we are capable of. Read this book if you want to elevate your mind and your heart.'

— **Daniel Priestley**, CEO, Dent Global, and author of *Entrepreneur Revolution*

'*The Gift* is an invitation, a challenge and a testament. It beckons us to join Zareen Roohi on her journey of compassion, courage with exuberance and love. It serves as a reminder that amidst life's tribulations, we possess the power to create waves that extend far beyond our imagination. As you embark on this poignant journey through Zareen's writings, may you be inspired, uplifted and compelled to embrace the gift of making a difference.'

— **Baroness Manzila Uddin**, Vice Chair, All Party Parliamentary Group on Population Development and Reproductive Rights, and the Women and Work Committee; Chair, All Party Parliamentary Group on Metaverse and Web 3

T0333633

'This is the story of an awe-inspiring mother driven to improve our planet and the lives of all its daughters. It's also a story about men: what it is to be the father, husband or son of such an amazing woman. To be sat down as a man with open eyes and ears to understand the harsh realities of period poverty, the healing power of tourmaline for endometriosis, brilliant entrepreneurship in the face of discrimination, and the power of love to find diamonds in the pieces of a broken heart.'
— **Brian Ballantyne**, author of *Confessions of a Working Father*, co-founder, Men for Inclusion, and former Senior Program Manager – Inclusion & Diversity, Amazon

'In a time when the world hungers for stories that will help us shape a new future, *The Gift* delivers a profound message of resilience and love. What sets this book apart is its ability to transcend the confines of a conventional autobiography. Zareen's words are enlightened by her multifaceted experience as a visionary entrepreneur, scholar and philanthropist. Her experiences and insights are not limited to any one sphere but encompass business, charity and philanthropy, and the universal pursuit of becoming a force for good. Her story is a testament to the indomitable spirit within us all, waiting to be ignited by the spark of will, inviting readers from all walks of life to reflect on their own journeys. This book is more than just a collection of words; it is a call

to action, an invitation to harness our pain and a reminder that our lives can be a gift to the world.'
— **Jeannie McGillivray**, co-founder and CEO, Remote.online, tech entrepreneur, author and investor

'This book is a true testament to a mother's unbound love for her child and how grief can be channelled to fuel positive change. I can only imagine the strength it took for Zareen to achieve everything she has in her daughter's memory but also that it took to put these words to paper, bringing Halimah's vision to life. Halimah would be very proud of what her mother and family have achieved. I know first-hand how difficult it can be to navigate this world as a woman, which makes what Zareen has achieved extraordinary. This book will serve as inspiration to anyone wanting to create a better world, and also offers support and strength for those that have suffered untimely grief.'
— **Nasreen Potter**, CREWS Regional Director, EMEA, Netflix

'Zareen's eloquent writing evokes vivid imagery that sears into your heart an indelible story of devastating loss transformed into miraculous empowerment, pure goodness and irresistible inspiration. *The Gift* is an invitation to overcome suffering and embrace a life of purpose.'
— **Diane Priestley**, journalist and author of *Over 50* and *Making a Difference*

'This book is a masterclass in vision, need, enormous hard work and determination for success. From a girls' school in Pakistan to developing inventive period products and working as a champion against period poverty and issues of discrimination, Zareen's life story will give inspiration to all those women who have a passion to create real change.'
— **Humera Khan**, consultant and researcher on Muslim Affairs, and co-founder, An-Nisa Society

'I thought I knew Zareen well, but after reading *The Gift*, I realised that I didn't. This book goes beyond autobiography. It is a story that elegantly weaves the themes of wellbeing, the environment and entrepreneurship. The book will take you on an emotional journey of sadness, anger, joy and hope and you will find new meaning for the word "gift". There are insightful examples and final actions to consider, which means that, time and time again, I will keep coming back to *The Gift* for inspiration.'
— **Dr Maggie Semple**, OBE, FCGI, Honorary Bencher of Middle Temple, co-founder and co-CEO, i-cubed

The Gift

One woman's journey
from tragedy to building
a global business for good

ZAREEN ROOHI AHMED

R^ethink

First published in Great Britain in 2023
by Rethink Press (www.rethinkpress.com)

© Copyright Zareen Roohi Ahmed

Contents

Foreword

The journey of life is never smooth. At some point, we all face obstacles that threaten to derail us from our path. These can come in the form of loss, grief, illness, financial difficulty or any number of other challenges. For many of us, these hurdles can seem insurmountable, causing us to lose hope and give up on our dreams. However, for Dr Zareen Roohi Ahmed, they were merely opportunities to grow, to learn and to make a difference.

In her book *The Gift*, Zareen shares her incredible story of resilience, determination and purpose. Her journey began with tragedy as she faced the unimaginable loss of her beloved daughter Halimah, but instead of succumbing to the pain and despair, Zareen chose to channel her grief into action. She established a charity in honour of her daughter and dedicated herself to helping women and girls around the world.

The approach Zareen took was to align with her purpose and follow a legacy she had planned to follow with her daughter, Halimah. She made a difference and continues to make a difference to women and girls around the world. She rebelled against the idea that she would disappear, that she would die inside, that she would not be able to cope. She rebelled against grief and brought meaning into her world.

Zareen's inherent belief system is a coping mechanism that clings to her conviction that this was meant to be for her. In some sense, it had to happen. Zareen created her own destiny and continues to do so. From tragedy, she emerged brighter than ever. She became a businesswoman with no previous business experience. She now uses her business to create good in the world and is expanding it as she steps into her social entrepreneurial status.

Through her company Gift Wellness, Zareen revolutionised the fem-care industry by creating a menstrual product that was not only safe and effective, but also sustainable and infused with the healing properties of tourmaline. It soon became the best-kept secret of the industry as it rose to popularity through word of mouth by endometriosis sufferers. She took her vision and turned it into a successful business, distributing her products to independent stores, larger high-street chains, and online retailers like Amazon.

Zareen didn't stop there. She used her platform to establish the Gift Wellness Foundation, a registered charity dedicated to eliminating period poverty and supporting women in crisis. Her irrepressible passion for this work led her to create a groundbreaking community-led app to tackle period poverty called Period Angels™, which she designed while sitting in a hotel room in Beirut during a deployment to distribute period products to women in Syrian refugee camps. She then developed a training consultancy using virtual reality (VR) technology to help organisations create more female-friendly workplaces and set up a simple process to enable employers to provide free menstrual products to their female staff and clients.

In *The Gift*, Zareen takes us on a journey of self-discovery, innovation and social entrepreneurship. She shares her highs and lows, from the initial stages of product development to the challenges of bootstrapping a business and establishing a charity from scratch. She teaches us that our work can be our solace, that giving and charitable work are the best of healers and can be integrated with running a business and making a profit. She shows us how we can reinvent ourselves in the face of adversity and turn tragedy into triumph.

Zareen's story is an impactful reminder that we all have the power to create change in the world.

Whether it's through business, charity or simply helping those around us, we can all make a difference. Zareen's journey is proof that with determination, purpose and a belief in oneself, anything is possible.

As you read *The Gift*, I encourage you to reflect on your own journey. What obstacles have you faced and how have you overcome them? What gifts have you been given and how have you used them to make a difference? Zareen's story is an inspiration to us all, and I am honoured to have the privilege of introducing her book to you.

Dr Sam Collins
CEO and founder, Aspire for Equality

Introduction

The Gift is my captivating journey of transformation, traversing the realms of heartache to illuminate the path of hope. Resonating deeply with readers from all walks of life, my story is not just a memoir; rather, it serves as a roadmap for effecting positive change in the world.

This book is an indispensable companion for those yearning to shape a brighter future, whether through entrepreneurship, philanthropy or simply by becoming a beacon of goodwill. *The Gift* transcends the boundaries of a conventional autobiography, embracing the facets of transformation, resilience and benevolence. My story will resonate profoundly with individuals who have experienced upheaval or hardship, while my experiences will inspire readers to channel their pain into positive action.

My entrepreneurial insights provide a deep understanding of the intricacies, pitfalls and opportunities entwined with the creation of a social enterprise. With my expertise in establishing charitable projects, I offer valuable guidance to those aspiring to make a transformative impact in the world while lacking a clear starting point. Moreover, my Gift-branded products serve as a revelation for individuals grappling with menstrual health concerns, as they have emerged as a game-changer for women worldwide, particularly those contending with endometriosis and other menstrual sensitivities.

As an entrepreneur, I strive to be forward-thinking and innovative, drawing from a diverse range of experiences and fields of expertise. Holding a PhD in multiculturalism, specialising in women's rights, I have spent over twenty-five years honing my skills in various senior roles. From spearheading urban regeneration projects to representing Britain on foreign office delegations as the chief executive officer (CEO) of the British Muslim Forum (BMF), I bring a multifaceted background to the table. However, it is my role as the founder and CEO of Gift Wellness – a social enterprise offering an award-winning range of natural toiletries, including vegan shampoo bars and menstrual products – that has had the most profound impact on women's lives.

Through Gift Wellness, I have been able to donate millions of menstrual products to homeless and refugee women, food banks and schools. In addition, the Gift Wellness Foundation is a registered charity dedicated to eradicating period poverty. This book describes my transformative journey from the depths of grief to social entrepreneurial success, chronicling the creation of my revolutionary menstrual products, the development of a thriving business and the establishment of a charitable foundation.

What to expect from this book

Chapter 1 introduces my tale of loss and how I harnessed my grief as a catalyst for action. It explores the concept of turning tragedy into triumph and using my love for my daughter, Halimah, as a driving force for positive change. My loss propelled me on a path to forge a lasting legacy in her name. Determined to create a social enterprise offering natural and sustainable toiletries benefiting women worldwide, I found myself simultaneously dedicated to the noble cause of eradicating period poverty.

Chapter 2 delves into my expedition of product development, unravelling the issues I sought to address, such as the hazards of toxic products, environmental concerns and the predicament of period poverty. It elucidates the distinctive qualities of tourmaline, the key ingredient in my menstrual pads, setting them apart from other products in the market. It unearths the profound emotional motivations underpinning my creations, drawing from intimate stories of women grappling with endometriosis, and reveals my unwavering commitment to crafting natural, sustainable and non-toxic products. The chapter also unravels the challenges I confronted in sourcing the finest ingredients and collaborating with manufacturers to meet my exacting standards.

Despite the obstacles I encountered, Gift Wellness rapidly amassed a devoted following of customers who resonated with the company's unwavering commitment to natural, sustainable products and social responsibility. Chapter 3 describes my marketing and branding knowledge, combined with my ability to flex my approach in an ever-changing landscape. This proved pivotal in propelling the business to success, as I tirelessly endeavoured to foster a strong, recognisable brand cherished by its clientele.

Chapter 4 brings us to the establishment of the Gift Wellness Foundation, a registered charity dedicated to combating period poverty and improving the lives of women worldwide. In this chapter, I divulge my strategies and the challenges I faced in tackling period poverty in the UK, highlighting the dearth of political support for the cause. I talk about the beneficiaries the Gift Wellness Foundation works tirelessly to serve, including homeless women, refugees, schoolgirls, women on low incomes and women's projects.

This chapter also unravels events unfolding during the Covid lockdown, encompassing the heightened demand from food banks and the loss of retailers. With Gift Wellness's unwavering commitment to donating free menstrual products for every pack sold, the period poverty initiative gained newfound momentum through the Foundation during the pandemic. The number of donations doubled from 3 to 6 million products within two years.

Additionally, I recount my deployment to Lebanon in August 2022, where I personally distributed menstrual products to women in Syrian and Palestinian refugee camps. This experience served as a catalyst for deeper understanding regarding the plight of displaced women. Between my visits to the camps, I dedicated my time to developing a community-led app called Period Angels™, designed to address period poverty, an endeavour that came to fruition with the app's launch in 2023. This chapter underscores the paramount significance of the Gift Wellness Foundation's work and the continued support required to propel the charity's mission forward.

Chapter 5 revolves around the themes of innovation, growth and marketing. I remain resolute in my commitment to stay ahead of the curve as Gift Wellness and the Foundation continue their expansion. Recognising the rapidly changing landscape of the world, I acknowledge that staying at the forefront of innovation is imperative to continue effecting positive change.

One area where I perceive immense potential for innovation lies in the environmental impact of products. With growing consumer concerns surrounding plastic usage in personal-care items, I endeavour to address this issue head-on. This led to the conception of the Plastic-Free Bathroom campaign, urging consumers to transition to plastic-free personal-care products. Gift Wellness stands as a trailblazing brand offering a range of plastic-free items, all meticulously crafted using pure essential oils and Epsom salts, encased in plastic-free paper packaging.

Furthermore, Chapter 5 recognises the possibilities for innovation in addressing menstrual-health issues faced by schoolgirls and women in the workplace. I have observed the discrimination and stigma many women encounter in their professional lives due to natural bodily functions such as menstruation, pregnancy and menopause – challenges that hinder their career prospects. To address this matter, I introduced my pioneering training consultancy, Female Friendly Workplaces, leveraging VR technology to simulate various scenarios. This empowers employers and teams to step into the shoes of women, comprehending the hurdles they face while balancing their jobs with their reproductive health.

Finally, the chapter explores the evolving landscape of marketing, from traditional methods to the emergence of social media, influencers and artificial intelligence (AI). It serves as a testament to the power of innovation and the ever-evolving nature of marketing in achieving goals and making a lasting impact on the world.

The final chapter of *The Gift* reflects on the invaluable lessons I've gleaned throughout my journey and presents a framework for attaining success while effecting positive change in the world. I underscore the significance of pushing boundaries, making a positive impact and remaining steadfast to personal values, while fusing business acumen with compassion to forge a more socially conscious future. Moreover, I emphasise the essential need to embrace the transformative power of kindness in the realm of business.

My story stands as an inspirational testament to the indomitable spirit of an individual, showcasing how determination and vision can truly shape the world. Through my own journey of resilience, innovation and giving back, I exemplify the potential to overcome adversity and create a lasting legacy that benefits others. *The Gift* transcends the confines of a traditional memoir; it stands as an invaluable guidebook for all those who yearn to effect positive change in the world.

In conclusion, *The Gift* is a wellspring of inspiration, empowering readers to embrace their dreams, overcome challenges and make a meaningful impact on the world. My first-hand experiences while navigating the intricate landscapes of creating a social enterprise offer an indispensable compass for individuals seeking to make a difference in the world, but who are uncertain of where to begin. Moreover, the book highlights the vital importance of menstrual health and period dignity for women across the globe. My Gift-branded products stand as game-changers and my work with the Gift Wellness Foundation shines as a beacon of hope, addressing period poverty and improving the lives of women everywhere.

Allow *The Gift* to serve as a gentle reminder that each one of us possesses the power to effect positive change in the world, becoming agents of transformation. Embark on this remarkable journey and uncover the profound significance of *The Gift* in your own life.

ONE

From Tragedy To Purpose

'The wound is the place where the light enters you.'
— Rumi[1]

In the crushing wake of a parent's deepest dread becoming real, I found myself shattered and aimless. Yet rather than succumbing to the suffocating grip of anguish and despair, I made a deliberate choice to rise from the ashes of my sorrow. With my grief serving as a raw and potent catalyst, I breathed life into a charity that would not only commemorate my precious daughter, but also echo our joint passion for offering succour to others.

This chapter, which chronicles my initial voyage towards healing, is about manifesting something luminous amid the ruinous devastation of grief.

It's about harnessing inner fortitude to forge ahead, even as the world crumbled around me. It's about the alchemy of turning heartbreak into triumph, repurposing my agony to carve a difference in the world. This is more than a narrative; it's a testament to my journey from despair's depths to hope's heights, and the enduring legacy that my daughter's memory has bequeathed me.

From celebration of unity to a devastating tragedy

As we journeyed away from the resounding buzz of the ExCel Centre in London, following a whirlwind weekend immersed in the Global Peace and Unity (GPU) event, my gaze instinctively drifted back to the rear seat of the car. The vision of my two children nestled there, my seventeen-year-old son Faizaan and nineteen-year-old daughter Halimah, slumbering peacefully with their heads leaning on each other, flooded my heart with pride and a sense of tranquillity.

Ash, my husband, and I exchanged a silent smile of shared appreciation, enamoured by the tableau of familial warmth behind us. The soothing melodies of Outlandish, a Danish nasheed band Halimah held dear, swirled from the CD player, evoking a bout of nostalgia. I found myself lost in the memory of the siblings sharing a hearty laugh about how Halimah had been approached by the band for directions to the stage at the event, and how she'd blushed and grinned as they trailed behind her through the exhibition hall.

The weekend at the GPU event had been a marvellous yet exhausting whirl. As the CEO of the BMF, a position I had been sought for by a board of respected Muslim religious leaders, I was honoured to present at the event. The BMF was conceived in the aftermath of the July 2005 London bombings, its purpose steadfast: to build bridges between Britain's Muslim community, the media, the government and society at large. As an intermediary, the BMF aims to stimulate dialogue and understanding among diverse communities.

Raised in the West Midlands in a predominantly white community, I have an eclectic background that spans graphic design, urban regeneration, philanthropy and government-backed initiatives, but I considered my tenure at BMF, entailing substantial responsibilities, as the apex of my career journey thus far. From representing the nation overseas to fostering relationships among varied communities, to intervening as a pacifier during bomb scares or comparable crises on behalf of the Muslim community, I found the role demanding, but immeasurably rewarding.

As I savoured the sight of my children in peaceful slumber, I was filled with a profound sense of gratification. The pride was not merely a reflection of my children's accomplishments, but a testament to the role I had played in fostering a more harmonious and inclusive society. My affiliation with the BMF was more than a professional commitment; it was an impassioned calling. A platform to effect change, to contribute to the collective good. I was unswerving in my resolve to play my part in constructing a society where every individual would be heard, where a sense of belonging would be universal.

As we navigated through the quiet roads towards Derby, gratitude enveloped me for my family, for my fulfilling work and the chance to make a positive impact on the world.

Defying conventions

Despite my upbringing in a devout Muslim family, the juxtaposition of my birthplace and childhood in the West Midlands had instilled a decidedly English essence in me. This had been evident in my sensibilities and lifestyle, creating a unique balance between the religious teachings I inherited and the cultural norms I absorbed. When I was summoned for an interview for the role of CEO at the BMF, scheduled at an office in the rear of the Leicester Mosque, it was not without a flutter of nervous anticipation. Venturing professionally into the religious sector was uncharted territory for me.

Five trustees faced me in a crescent formation, their austere demeanours strikingly noticeable. Two large men in long sherwani jackets over white tunics dominated the room from a central sofa, flanked by the others seated in armchairs, each sporting distinctive headgear – towering brown or grey Nehru style hats, lambs' wool topis or white turbans meticulously wound around hats. Their varied facial hair styles resembled a beard exposition, from silver-grey to white, henna-dyed terracotta orange and a relatively short jet-black one. The singular clean-shaven figure among them was the BMF chairman, Khurshid Ahmed. His reassuring presence was a comfort, particularly as he had been the one who'd head-hunted me and extended the job invitation.

Being the first woman ever interviewed, let alone appointed to helm the BMF, I couldn't help but feel slightly alien. Yet, my mission was clear: to share my vision of refurbishing the British Muslim community's image, tainted following the 7/7 attacks. As the interview unfolded, I found myself repeating answers in Urdu to ensure comprehension. The trustees would occasionally discuss me in my presence, enquiring about my marital connections or my husband's occupation.

The abrupt Azaan (call to prayer) led them to dash off mid-conversation, returning ten minutes later to recommence the interview. Then came the food – a spice-laden endurance test, leaving my face aflame, my nose running and my fingertips tainted with turmeric from the array of curries. Hardly the ideal interview impression, yet despite this unorthodox encounter, I was granted the position.

I had made history, becoming the first woman to lead a national Muslim organisation not only in Britain, but likely in Europe as well. My dual identity, as a devout Muslim and an English woman, facilitated a redefined image of the Muslim community during volatile times, projecting a moderate, inclusive face to the world.

This appointment initiated an exciting chapter in my life, laden with steep challenges and diverse responsibilities. I had to become media-ready, capable of responding in television newsroom studios and on radio platforms to bomb scares or controversies related to Muslims. Khurshid embraced me, becoming my mentor with the warmth and protectiveness of a big brother. As he is a consummate orator and master of managing people, his tutelage became invaluable as I absorbed an immense wealth of knowledge and skills from him.

My role encompassed forging relationships with influential figures and speaking at international events, from the United States and Canada to the Far East, Pakistan, Turkey and various parts of Europe. From engaging with senior ministers to working closely with mosques, women's groups, local police and navigating press scrutiny, I found the role multi-faceted and deeply fulfilling.

A shattered peace

The GPU event was a prestigious occasion, orchestrated by the Islam Channel, with a noble goal of promoting unity and camaraderie among leaders from diverse faiths. Renowned figures such as the Archbishop of Canterbury and the Chief Rabbi have graced the stage, delivering profound messages on unity and the importance of harmonious coexistence. As a chosen speaker, I was thrilled that my family – Halimah, Faizaan and Ash – joined me for the weekend, supporting me from the front row as I addressed an awe-inspiring crowd of over 20,000 attendees.

Upon our late-night return home, the familiar warmth of the kitchen enveloped me, soon joined by Halimah's comforting presence. Her customary goodnight hug, combined with her words of pride in my work, kindled a rush of love within me. I kissed her face while thanking her and reflected on her invaluable contribution to the event's success, and how her management of our stand and volunteers was a testament to her maturity and confidence.

Her arms still wrapped around me, she shared her plans for the next day – a university trip to work on an assignment. Just six weeks prior, Halimah had embarked on her dream degree course, studying International Relations and Global Politics at Nottingham Trent University, with the aim of specialising in

Third World Development. She was especially excited for an opportunity in The Gambia during the second year of her course, where she would work on crucial environmental and water projects.

Halimah and Zareen, Aug 2007

Charity work had been a cornerstone of Halimah's life since her primary school days, a heartfelt commitment that extended into her teenage years. She regularly sold home-baked fairy cakes at school to generate funds for various causes, supported UNICEF, and proudly displayed certificates awarded by the Red Cross and other charities for her persistent efforts. Halimah and I shared a pact, an agreement to work together following her graduation on charity projects and social enterprise. Our conversations about future plans would be peppered with her light-hearted musings about how we would have to find her a wealthy man to marry, since her chosen path was more heart-rich than money-rich.

The following day dawned like any other. I left for work, Faizaan for sixth form, and Ash set off for his day. Halimah, snug in her dreams, would rise later for her university commitment. Midway through a meeting in my Derby office at around 2.45pm, I received a call from Halimah, confirming she was on her way to the campus and including a gentle reminder to pick up Faizaan at 4pm as she wouldn't return in time. Little did I know then that these fleeting moments of routine conversation would become the last shared words between Halimah and me.

The night Halimah vanished remains seared into my memory, a stark, haunting echo of pain that reverberates even today. After an otherwise ordinary day had unfolded, I anticipated the reassuring chime of my daughter's message. As the clock ticked past 7pm, a growing unease began to gnaw at me; Halimah would ordinarily have texted by then, either asking about dinner or sharing snippets from her day. Yet, my phone maintained a disconcerting silence.

In our rising anxiety, Ash and I reached out to her friends, hoping to hear her voice or at least locate her whereabouts. Our efforts yielded nothing but a void. By 10pm, with our hearts pounding and our minds consumed by a fear we dared not voice, we made the call to the police.

They initiated an immediate search, scouring local hospitals for any hint of her presence. Yet Halimah was nowhere to be found. Each attempt to reach her on her phone was met with the abrupt impersonal tone of voicemail. As the night wore on, we grappled with a profound sense of helplessness and raw distress, each passing minute deepening our despair.

As dawn broke on the next day, Ash and I found ourselves roaming the campus of Halimah's university, frantic desperation gripping us. We presented her picture to every passing student, every staff member we met, praying that someone might have seen her. Across the breadth of the university, we disseminated 'missing' posters, each one a silent plea for help. Yet, as the day wore on, our efforts felt futile. We returned home, exhausted and desolate, the path forward shrouded in uncertainty.

Around 3pm, we received a call from our nephew. He alerted us to a news story on the BBC that sent a chill through our spines. The report told of a young woman's body, discovered just streets away from our house. Despite our instinctual protestations that it couldn't be Halimah, we knew we had to investigate. As we neared the scene, our view was flooded with police cars and a house ominously shielded by a stark white forensic tent. The location teemed with officers and curious locals.

Our nephew navigated the car into a parking spot nearby, while Ash, trying to spare me the sight of what might lie ahead, suggested I stay behind. He ventured with our nephew to the car park just across from the cordoned-off house. Moments later, Ash reappeared at the edge of the car park; he seemed to be staggering, his face ashen and dazed. The sight struck a chilling chord in my heart, and I knew without words what had transpired.

Pushing past my dread, I made my way to the car park, but halfway there, my legs buckled beneath me. Ash darted forward to keep me from falling. A police officer, sensing our distress, approached. Through a whirlwind of fear and gasping breaths, we managed to relay our story – our daughter was missing, and the red Rover 25 in the car park was hers.

We found ourselves ensconced in the cold interior of a police car as an officer took a photo of Halimah from my purse to the crime scene. When he returned, his face betrayed the dreadful news before his words could – the young woman's body was, to the best of his knowledge, that of our daughter. We were ushered to the police station to provide our statements, each word a painful puncture in the veil of disbelief we clung to.

When we finally returned home, it was teeming with the compassionate presence of our family. My older brother took on the heart-wrenching task of going with an officer to formally identify the body. The rest of us sat in a strained silence, nursing the hope that perhaps, just perhaps, there had been a catastrophic mistake.

Our fragile hope was shattered when my brother returned, confirming the unthinkable. It was Halimah.

Confronting the unthinkable

The following day demanded a conscious choice from me to keep living, to keep breathing. Mustering the strength to climb out of bed felt akin to climbing a mountain. Yet I knew I needed to be a pillar of strength for my family, to bear the weight of our shared grief.

Over the days that followed, a horrific reality began to solidify. Halimah had been targeted by a man suffering from mental health issues, who had, in a twisted culmination of his obsession, taken her life before ending his own.

I make the deliberate choice not to mention his name for two reasons. Firstly, I refuse to let his identity become entwined with my daughter's memory. Secondly, I perceive him as a victim of his own circumstances, and out of respect for his struggles and the pain his family must bear, I choose not to add to their anguish.

The man who took my daughter from us was an Iraqi Kurd, an asylum seeker who had been witness to the unrelenting horrors of war in his home country. Plagued by post-traumatic stress disorder and deep-seated depression, he was a soul in turmoil. His mental health nurse, during the subsequent coroner's inquest, revealed that he had confessed to harbouring an unhealthy obsession with a young woman, and had even admitted to a volatile temper that he feared he could not control, potentially endangering those around him or himself.

Despite him having a history of arrests for violent conduct and other transgressions, his case was handled with a bewildering lack of urgency. He was shunted between the police, the Border Agency and the mental-health services, with his increasingly dangerous mental state largely disregarded. Alarmingly, in the weeks preceding the tragedy, Derbyshire Mental Health Services had ignored three separate Section 2 orders, failing to commit him to psychiatric care. The coroner later noted in the inquest that had they taken the required action, Halimah may very well still have been with us.

In a chilling turn of events, he had managed to procure Halimah's phone number from a mutual acquaintance and had called her on that fateful morning. He persuaded her to stop by his residence on Moore Street for a quick conversation. Being the ever-helpful soul she was, Halimah had intended it to be a brief stop before her university commitments, as was evidenced by her belongings and phone being discovered later in her car.

However, the horrifying forensic evidence painted a different picture of what ensued at his residence. Bruising on her arms and wrists bore testimony to a fierce struggle and her forced entry into the house. She had been struck, either by a blunt object or a forceful punch, resulting in significant brain trauma that left her unconscious. Following this, she was smothered with a pillow. Tragically, within two hours, the man who had perpetrated this monstrous act took his own life in the same room.

Halimah's funeral took place four days later at the Jamia Mosque in Derby. It was a solemn Friday that witnessed nearly 2,000 attendees congregating to honour her through speeches and poems. In a show of remarkable courage, Faizaan sang one of Halimah's favoured nasheeds. The gathering was a mosaic of distant relatives and community members who watched, somewhat bewildered, as various delegations representing different sects and faiths arrived from London to pay their respects.

As the funeral rites concluded, I felt as though my very being shifted into autopilot, a crucial shield enabling me to steer through the tumultuous waves of the days that lay ahead. The cloak of stoicism enveloped me for six long months, until one day it could no longer contain my suppressed sorrow, which burst forth in a torrent of tears that lasted hours, only ceasing when I was teetering on the edge of collapse.

Throughout that initial period, maintaining composure was vital, especially for Faizaan, while condolences and heartfelt tributes cascaded in from my network and the BMF community. Elegant potted orchids arrived from the Home Office Minister, and the gentle timbre of former Bishop Riah's voice from Jerusalem enveloped me during a consoling phone call; he had met Halimah just days before at the GPU event. Notably, Sadiq Khan MP, who now holds the esteemed office of Mayor of London, reached out during his Hajj pilgrimage in Mecca, Saudi Arabia. Alongside him was his close friend, Asad Ahmad, a respected BBC London newsreader. Their words, infused with compassion, conveyed the special prayers they had offered for Halimah and our family amid the sacred air of Mecca.

In the aftermath of the funeral, our faith was our fortress. I know that my belief in God, the afterlife and the concept of divine predestination, or 'Qadr' as we refer to it in Islam, is what saw me through the darkest days. The conviction that our separation was temporary and all part of a preordained plan lent me peace, solace and acceptance. It also fuelled a pressing desire within me to strive to realise Halimah's dreams.

Launch of The Halimah Trust

In the days following the funeral, I resolved to establish a charity in Halimah's honour. It was then that I recalled a bank account Halimah and I had once opened, called The Halimah Trust. It seemed an undeniable signal that we should retain this name for the charity.

Bill Marwood, who became one of our esteemed trustees, devised the strapline, 'Keeping dreams alive', which poignantly encapsulated our mission's core. I drafted the registration papers for the charity and personally handed them to Dame Suzi Leather, then Chair of the Charity Commission, a friend whose warmth and compassion were invaluable during this trying time. A few weeks later, the charity was officially established. Our son, Faizaan, bravely voiced his aspiration to head The Halimah Trust as its first chair, an ambition we fervently endorsed, believing it would provide a constructive and purposeful avenue for his focus. At the tender age of eighteen, when the charity was officially registered, he became the youngest chairperson of any UK-based charity, an achievement that gave us immense pride. His youthful dynamism earned him the spotlight in the subsequent monthly newsletter of the Charity Commission, and as the year unfolded, he won several awards for his exemplary leadership qualities among the youth.

However, despite our aspirations, we acknowledged our lack of practical experience in international aid work. Thus, we opted to extend an open invitation for partnership proposals to established charities known for their on-ground efforts in developing countries. Our vision was not just to finance a project, but also to immerse ourselves, as far as possible, in the delivery of the aid.

The response was heartening, with proposals pouring in from organisations like Oxfam and Islamic Relief among others. However, it was the initiative proposed by Muslim Hands, a Nottingham-based charity renowned for its work to build schools in Pakistan, that instantaneously resonated with us.

Muslim Hands presented its work on a school in Wazirabad, a facility dedicated to supporting orphaned and disadvantaged boys. Yet, it quickly became apparent that a corresponding school for girls was conspicuously absent in the area. This situation particularly struck a chord with us, as Wazirabad neighboured the city of Sialkot where my parents were from. There were hundreds of orphan girls in desperate need of schooling, many of whom were tragically rendered homeless due to the catastrophic earthquake in Kashmir the previous year. Our dear Halimah had been a passionate fundraiser for these very victims. Consequently, the prospect of this project resonated with us profoundly, and it beckoned us on many levels.

As my tenure at the BMF approached its two-year threshold, I chose to relinquish my role as CEO. The recognition that I could not consistently guarantee the level of commitment that the position demanded – a daily embodiment of robustness to tackle pressing issues and a constant readiness for media interaction – was born out of self-awareness rather than resignation. My survival strategy was to focus my energies on the charity.

I've never believed in coincidences or chance. I firmly believe that when a vision is nurtured with as much passion as Halimah exhibited, it must inevitably come to fruition. The selfless love and energy for helping others that she radiated as a young girl created the reality that we see today.

There were countless serendipitous moments that graced our journey, instances that retrospectively appear laden with profound meaning. One such incident remains etched in my memory, occurring five years prior to Halimah's untimely departure, when she was just fourteen.

My father and I found ourselves obligated to journey to Pakistan to visit my ailing aunt, his sister, in Karachi. Traditionally inseparable, my parents rarely ventured without the other's company; my father would often express his wish to depart this world alongside my mother. However, she had recently undergone a cataract surgery, rendering her unfit for travel. Given my aunt's critical condition, my father had no choice but to proceed, although the prospect of solo travel was discomforting.

Recognising the potential for emotional strain, I offered to accompany him. It marked our first long-distance voyage together, an experience I deeply treasure. We took an Emirates flight via Dubai, and my father's Sialkoti Punjabi humour kept me in high spirits throughout the journey.

On the aeroplane, we found ourselves seated next to a pair of newlyweds. They were on the receiving end of the cabin crew's special attention, treated to cake and drinks throughout the flight.

In a conspiratorial whisper, my father turned to me and quipped in Punjabi, 'Mona, I reckon the next time your mother and I venture to Pakistan, I'll declare us as newlyweds too.' His jest ignited a flurry of laughter, the joyous echoes of which continue to warm my heart in the recollection.

Fortuitously, my cousin Arshad, the eldest son of my ailing aunt, was employed at Jinnah International Airport in Karachi. His position granted us privilege as he ensured we bypassed the bustling queues and rigorous security checks, directly escorting us to his vehicle. As a British-born child, I hadn't enjoyed the experience of growing up alongside my cousins. We were six siblings, four sisters and two brothers, yet our father's financial constraints had hindered any possibility of holidaying together in Pakistan, despite my parents' deep-rooted desire for and emphasis on maintaining our cultural ties to our ancestral land. It was only in my early twenties that I embarked on my first trip to Pakistan.

Meeting my cousins for the first time elicited a sense of profound sentiment. Beyond our evident physical resemblances, I could discern echoes of my siblings and myself in their voices, mannerisms, postures and even hand gestures. Arshad's demeanour was strikingly reminiscent of my older brother, Sohail. While the experience filled me with joy and gratitude, a tinge of melancholy clouded these emotions due to the absence of the opportunity for shared childhood memories, now lost forever.

During my stay, while my father kept vigil by my aunt's bedside, Arshad and I would engage in profound discussions about work and the prevailing issues in Pakistan. An idea began to germinate during these conversations – we could join forces in charity work. With Arshad possessing an unoccupied property, we envisioned transforming it into a school for the local underprivileged children.

Upon returning to England, I shared this initiative with Halimah. She responded enthusiastically.

'Mum, you know that that's the sort of work I want to do when I grow up, so can you name the charity after me?'

The next day, we went to the bank together and opened an account called The Halimah Trust. Unfortunately, due to bureaucratic hurdles in Pakistan, the Karachi project was unable to materialise at the time, leaving the bank account dormant. Following Halimah's passing, the memory of that dormant account resurfaced. In retrospect, I realised that naming the account in Halimah's honour signified a portent of something far more profound and impactful than I could have ever fathomed.

With the registration of the charity and the decision to pursue our first flagship project, our focus shifted towards designing the girls' school and raising the necessary funds. Trustee meetings became vital strategic huddles, charting our course towards the ambitious £150,000 target. Our project manager, Yasrab Shah from Muslim Hands, was an esteemed scholar whose empathetic guidance proved instrumental during challenging junctures. His unwavering support, eloquent recitations and insightful reflections drawn from prophetic teachings bolstered our morale and became indispensable during fundraising events. Notably, my husband Ash and son Faizaan were privileged to join Yasrab in an adventurous endeavour, scaling Mount Kilimanjaro and successfully raising substantial funds for the Halimah School of Excellence.

In the year that followed Halimah's departure, we bore witness to the incredible resilience and magnanimity of humanity. Having spent two decades living and working in Derby, we were profoundly touched by the overwhelming surge of empathy and support from every quarter of the city. Our shared tragedy seemed to galvanise the community, and the resultant outpouring of generosity frequently moved us to tears.

Owing to the high-profile nature of the case, the media remained keenly attuned to our efforts, meticulously documenting the endeavours of a bereaved family striving to build a school as an enduring tribute to their beloved daughter. This widespread coverage attracted donations from far and wide; not just from our local community, but from diverse communities across the country and beyond its borders.

Catharsis through creativity

The prospect of confronting the first summer without Halimah filled me with woeful apprehension. Our nephew, in an act of compassion, convinced Ash, Faizaan and me to accompany him and his family to Turkey. He reasoned that a change of scene and a break away from home could soothe our sorrow-laden hearts.

It was there, sitting with the sea as my sole companion, that I found tears streaming down my face, echoing the ebb and flow of the tide. My heart replayed all the cherished holiday moments we'd shared, every laugh, every silence. I was strangled with the painful realisation that I didn't want to be there without her; I didn't want to be *anywhere* without her.

The torrent of emotions threatened to consume my very being, gnawing at my insides with a primal intensity. It was then that I began transcribing my feelings, an act that served as a balm to my open wounds. I felt as though I was transferring the weight of the world from my shoulders on to the blank canvas of the page before me. Tears intermingled with the ink, yet I persevered, and despite their simplicity, those words faithfully mirrored my deepest love and intent.

Within an hour, my sentiments had created a poem, catalysed by my tearful determination, the warmth of the surroundings, the rhythm of the lapping waves and the distant melody of Turkish music. That metamorphosed into the lyrics of a song. Clutching these lyrics, my stomach a riot of butterflies, I ascended to our hotel room and sang the song to Ash and Faizaan, my voice shaking with the strain of raw emotion.

I then proposed to Faizaan we perform it as a charity single, to support the Halimah School. I believed it would also serve as a catharsis for his own suppressed emotions. He accepted the challenge with a resolve that mirrored my own. Exactly a year later, we returned to the GPU event, armed with CDs of our song, 'One Day', and Faizaan ready to perform on the main stage.

The lyrics are:

Verse 1:
My love, love, pure and right,
Think of no one else, day and night.
All I see are your eyes, shining bright,
On my lips is your name I recite.

Chorus:
And I know that you'll never be far,
When I need you, you will be my friend.
And one day, we'll be together,
When our purpose is served in the end.

Verse 2:
When I, when I sleep at night,
And I pray for a single sight,
Of your face and your smile, full of light,
Arms around me, holding me so tight.

Chorus:
And I know that you'll never be far,
When I need you, you will be my friend.
And one day, we'll be together,
When our purpose is served in the end.

Verse 3:
Grateful, grateful for life,
Your example of struggle and strife,
How for others, you made sacrifice,
How the thought of it cuts like a knife.

Chorus:
And I know that you'll never be far,
When I need you, you will be my friend.
And one day, we'll be together,
When our purpose is served in the end.

Verse 4: (Urdu)
Teri Yaadon mein, jiyoonga,
Raat, din, tere naam pe.
Ek din, tere saath hoonga,
Ya Rab ke baag mein.

(Translation):
In your memory, I will persist,
Day and night, your name on my lips.
One day, with you, our fates entwined,
In God's garden, we will find.

Verse 5:
Oh God, God, help me fight
For the helpless and victims of plight,
I will struggle, with all of my might,
And Inshallah, be there by your side.

Chorus:
And I know that you'll never be far,
When I need you, you will be my friend.
And one day, we'll be together,
When our purpose is served in the end.
And one day, we'll be together,
When our purpose is served in the end.

Our cherished friend, Harj Dhanjal, a prodigious music producer who was immensely fond of Halimah, graciously extended his expertise to produce the song in his home studio. Faraz Yousufzai, another dear friend and colleague known for his captivating guitar playing, adorned the song with an enchantingly beautiful acoustic melody. As if the stars had aligned, Harj had a close friend who had previously worked as a video editor for the late celebrated Amy Winehouse. He generously volunteered to assemble a montage of images and footage that portrayed our story, thereby crafting a moving music video. This poignant tribute is still accessible on YouTube, under the title 'One Day Music Video – Faizaan Ahmed'.[2]

CD cover of 'One Day' charity single

Emergence of hope

In the landmark year of 2008, my father was the first of our family to visit the site of the budding Halimah School in Wazirabad. His voyage to the roots of our lineage marked the emergence of a dream into reality. As he returned, he unveiled his experiences, recounting how the very fields, which once echoed with his youthful laughter, were now the cradle of a beacon of knowledge – the Halimah School. His voice, heavy with sentiment, betrayed the tears he fought to withhold. He stood amazed, humbled by the divine orchestration of life that had led us back to Pakistan.

When Halimah's absence carved a hollow space in my heart, I sought solace in the familiarity of my childhood home in Dudley. No balm was quite as healing as the warmth of my father's arms around me. His presence was a tranquil shelter from the storm of my emotions. Whenever he would find me with tears streaming down my face, he would tenderly reassure me.

'Mona,' he would say, 'if tears had the power to change the fate, we would all unite to shed an ocean, enough to bring her back.'

Yet, beneath this resilient exterior was a heart that mirrored my own pain. The mere mention of Halimah's name would draw tears to his eyes, a testament to the bond between a grandparent and a grandchild.

In many respects, the grief borne by Halimah's grandparents was a burden even heavier than that of Ash, Faizaan and myself.

A few months after his visit to Wazirabad, my father was diagnosed with cancer. Despite our fervent hopes and prayers, by April 2009, he'd succumbed to the disease. The house was shrouded in grief, and though we tried our best to distract my mother, to offer her comfort and companionship, the sparkle in her eyes began to dim after my father's departure. A mere four years passed before she joined him, leaving us to grapple with their combined absence.

In the spring of 2011, marking three years since our charity was registered, my elder sister Tehsin, Ash, my mother and I ventured to Pakistan. Our purpose was the inauguration of the Halimah School of Excellence. Tehsin, the eldest among us, had been an unwavering pillar of support during the most tumultuous and heartrending times, from clasping my hand in solidarity during the coroner's inquest to standing by my side as we unveiled the school we had collectively built. Her maternal, protective love was an essential cornerstone of my journey.

Upon beholding the Halimah School of Excellence, I was struck by a surge of emotion. The building, symmetrical, adorned with patterns of pink and cream brickwork, bore Halimah's name in bold letters above the double-fronted entrance. It felt akin to visiting her, with her spirit palpably resonating in the very air surrounding the building. The overwhelming rush of emotion was intense, testing the steadiness of my feet.

Halimah School of Excellence, April 2011

Girls who had been orphaned arrived from across Pakistan, many from the earthquake-ravaged region of Kashmir where villages had vanished beneath merciless landslides. Among them, a young girl with a streak of white hair drew my attention. The stark contrast between that streak and the rest of her dark hair bespoke the unimaginable trauma and fear she had endured. These girls, each carrying stories of resilience, were given thorough medical checks and clean clothing, and introduced to their new homes and families – other girls of similar ages hailing from different parts of the country.

During the initial days, the girls appeared apprehensive of their new surroundings. Their pale faces and fleeting smiles spoke volumes of their uncertainty. However, as the days passed, the hushed whispers gave way to laughter and lively chatter. The girls began to bond as though they had known each other for years. Their complexions brightened, their eyes gleamed with newfound excitement and optimism as they navigated their vibrant school. When I looked into their eyes, it was as if Halimah's spirit gazed back at me.

'We are your daughters now, Zareen Sahiba,' they declared, vying for my attention and affection.

The official inauguration of the school took place on 15 April 2011, beneath an opulent marquee elegantly arranged within the verdant grounds behind the main building. As we made our way towards the marquee through the school's courtyard, we were drawn to a moment of solemn reverence. A gleaming brass plaque was unveiled, bearing an inscription that immortalised Halimah's dream – the very words she'd penned in her college application:

> 'I aim to go to university to study Third World Development and International Relations. This will enable me to find a job that will give me the opportunity to travel to different countries and help improve the environment and minimise poverty. In this way, I will fulfil my ambition to improve people's lives and make a difference in the world.'
> — **Halimah Ahmed**, 20 January 2005

This plaque stands as an enduring tribute to the noble aspirations of the soul for whom the school is named. Like an ethereal talisman, it will guide the Halimah School in its unwavering mission to be a force for goodness and transformation in the world. It will also serve as a gentle reminder for the students to invoke Halimah's memory in their morning assembly prayers.

For the official inauguration, the students had prepared performances that showcased Pakistan's diverse national attire, representing various regions of the country. Government officials praised the school's potential for the region, while Ash and I offered brief speeches. The day culminated in the release of nineteen white doves, symbolising each year of Halimah's life.

Zareen and her mother at Halimah's statement plaque, 2011

Morning assembly at Halimah School of Excellence

The creation of the Halimah School of Excellence transcended the fulfilment of a dream. It was an act of transforming profound grief into a beacon of positivity. Our aspiration was to etch a legacy in Halimah's name, with the school as its symbol. It was envisaged as a sanctuary where orphan girls could find not only shelter and education, but also love and support. This school was – and is – an homage to Halimah's benevolent spirit, her fervour for education, and a testament to the kindness of countless people, from family and friends to anonymous donors from around the globe. In unison, we managed to transmute a tragedy into a promise of hope.

Within three years of the inauguration of the Halimah School of Excellence, it became apparent that our endeavour was yielding tremendous results. The pupils were flourishing, not just academically, but holistically, as they embraced a future brimming with possibilities. This instilled in us the conviction that our mission had only just begun, and thus, the Halimah College was born to extend the reach of education and empowerment.

As I pen these words, the Halimah campus is pulsating with life, and the chorus of over 1,000 girls resonates with dreams, aspirations and the unwavering spirit of Halimah that continues to guide us forward. For every soul that played a part in this journey, my gratitude knows no bounds.

Envisioning empowerment
for women in crisis

Two days after the inauguration, ensconced within the confines of Lahore airport's lounge as we journeyed home, I allowed my thoughts to drift. The fundraiser for the Halimah School had concluded, marking the need for me to chart my course back to work. However, I was acutely aware of my desire to work independently, to maintain a ceaseless connection with the charity and, by extension, with Halimah herself. Amid these reflections, my hands reached for a copy of a magazine from the nearby coffee table, drawing me into an article detailing the plight of Syrian women in the Za'atari refugee camp.

The piece highlighted the stories of these women, many highly educated and possessing valuable skills, who had been compelled to abandon their homes with nothing but the clothes on their backs. Their existence was dominated by the perpetual fear of sexual abuse and the grim reality of making unthinkable sacrifices, such as trading sexual favours for food for their children. The article narrated how in the midst of this frightful existence, women coped with the lack of access to sanitary products combined with the scarcity of clean water. Refugee women had no choice but to tear strips off the bottom of the abayas (long dresses) they were wearing to fold up into makeshift sanitary pads, a situation which exacerbated rates of infection. The issue was receiving scant attention from aid organisations.

As I immersed myself in the harrowing narratives of these women, I was all at once jolted by a profound surge of emotion from the pit of my stomach. In retrospect, I can't be certain whether I physically rose from my seat in that moment, but I undoubtedly felt the sensation of standing. I saw myself distributing sanitary pads to these women and I realised this was my ensuing calling. What I was envisioning was my and Halimah's dream of working together to empower women, which ignited a flame in my heart; a flame I knew required action.

Sharing my new vision with my sister and husband, I met a bemused if not exasperated gaze. Regardless, I spent the entire homeward journey fervently jotting down notes on napkins and newspaper margins, consumed by the concept of funding sanitary-pad distributions in refugee camps through product sales. I understood that this fresh mission would be as daunting as the Halimah School endeavour, yet my resolve was unwavering. Seated on the plane, my mind rife with the possible challenges I would encounter, but motivated by the resilience and struggles of the Syrian women etched in the magazine pages, I felt a compelling need to ease their plight.

The subsequent weeks would witness me embarking on a new project, one that would once again stretch the limits of my determination and tenacity. However, I was primed for the challenge, acutely aware that my drive was fuelled by a purpose extending far beyond personal aspiration.

TWO

Revolutionising Women's Health

'Where there is ruin, there is hope for a treasure.'
— Rumi[3]

In embarking upon the healing odyssey that followed my personal tragedy, I yearned to honour Halimah's legacy with a creation that would enrich women's lives universally. A single aspiration coalesced: to cultivate change, to cultivate hope.

Chapter 2 chronicles this transformational journey, outlining each step from preliminary research through to the launch of a trailblazing menstrual product. It navigates through the quagmire of issues plaguing women's health – the insidious presence of toxic substances, crippling health concerns and the global crisis of period poverty. I unravel the scientific marvel encapsulated in my groundbreaking product – the precious mineral, tourmaline – illuminating its astounding benefits shared by customers who have found solace from afflictions like endometriosis. This chapter is more than just a narrative of innovation – it's a testament to the resilience of the human spirit, to my endeavour to transmute my loss into a beacon of hope that brightens the lives of others.

A new journey

Despite the lingering symptoms of jet lag, the day after my return from Pakistan, I remained steadfast in my mission to equip refugee women with vital menstrual products. Imbued with an unwavering resolve, a fire kindling within me, I flipped open my laptop, ready to commence my primary research.

It didn't take long for an unsettling reality to confront me: period poverty, a plague that extends its cold grip far beyond refugee camps and famine-stricken regions, was silently tormenting thousands of women in my home country of Britain. As I plunged further into this murky abyss, I came to understand a universal truth: where hardship looms over women, the spectre of period poverty is inevitably present.

Energised by the vision that now shaped my endeavour, I set my sights on the products I intended to offer. My digital exploration led me to several manufacturers dotted across Europe and to Alibaba, the vast Chinese trading nexus. Upon registering and placing orders for various sample packs of pads and ingredients from different firms, I stumbled upon a series of scholarly articles and scientific publications highlighting the dangerous toxicity lurking within ordinary menstrual products.

The startling revelation that the products I had relied on for so long harboured harmful chemicals, which were causing my monthly discomfort, struck me like a lightning bolt. It was this jarring epiphany that cemented my resolve to forge my own brand of menstrual pads that would harness the power of natural ingredients. In stark contrast to mainstream products, the ingredients of my pads would be transparently listed on the packaging, empowering my customers with the knowledge of what they were introducing to their bodies.

Regarding the business model, I found myself torn between the decision to finance the donation of pads to women caught in crises from my profits, or to seamlessly embed such charitable acts into the routine sales strategy. Trusting my instincts, I opted for the latter. For each pack sold, I pledged to donate pads to women grappling with barriers to accessing or affording menstrual products, both locally in Britain and globally.

The prospect was undoubtedly daunting; I was venturing into uncharted territory, devoid of any experience in establishing a business, much less innovating and manufacturing a new product. Yet, I was aware that my first step was relatively simple – download a rudimentary business plan template from the internet and distil my thoughts into succinct bullet points under each section.

Initially, the enormity of the undertaking was intimidating as it opened up a plethora of questions I hadn't yet explored. Whenever a new challenge began to cloud my vision, I would redirect my focus to the heart of my mission, visualising myself extending those vital pads into the hands of women in need. This image would galvanise me, providing a surge of determination and urgency that propelled me through the operational and technical tasks that were integral to inching me closer to my aspiration.

As a visually oriented individual, I frequently employed mind maps as tools to dissect different strategies. Instead of merely jotting down notes, I brought my journals to life with diagrams – an array of boxes linked by arrows, clouds and stars marking crucial action points. This approach allowed me to comprehend the entirety of a meeting or personal note at a single glance, circumventing the need to comb through dense paragraphs. Crucially, creating mind maps and mood boards proved to be an invaluable tool in visually expressing my vision and effectively conveying my purpose.

For a span of nearly eighteen months, my life was fully steeped in this journey of research and product development. Grasping the nuances of importing, amassing samples of materials and ingredients, engaging in dialogue with manufacturers – these tasks became the rhythm of my existence. This pursuit was a haven from my grief, and whenever the spectre of sorrow threatened to engulf me, I would swiftly divert my focus to the next milestone in my blueprint.

Despite the strides I was making, there were instances when Halimah's absence cast a profound shadow over me, piercing even the most jubilant moments. While the obvious milestones like birthdays and holidays undeniably stung, it was often the mundane quotidian moments that magnified the void left by my daughter. Hearing music she would have adored, such as Adele's *19* – an album that, in a twist of fate, debuted just after her departure – would instigate a flood of melancholy. I'd catch myself envisioning us taking lengthy car rides, belting out our favourite tunes. The final episode of *Prison Break* – one we were supposed to watch together, but which aired on the night of her disappearance – remains unwatched to this day, a tribute to the bond we shared.

Reflecting on the technological leaps since Halimah's time, I am met with reminders of all the developments she never had the chance to witness. Her missing out on the meteoric rise of smartphone technology – now a practically indispensable part of our lives – feels particularly poignant. The fact that she lived in an era of iPods, never experiencing the advent of smartphones, is surreal. In a world where smartphones are a pervasive presence, this underlines the dramatic technological progression since she left us. Yet, amid the twinge of her absence, I treasure memories, finding comfort in the enduring echo of Halimah's spirit within them.

In the grips of such pain, I would channel my energy into my venture, driving myself to conquer new milestones. I garnered ideas from an eclectic mix of sources, endlessly brainstorming and crafting mind maps, always seeking novel avenues for enhancing my product and refining my business model. The journey was slow, fraught with moments of frustration, but I was steadfast in my resolve to persevere.

In retrospect, it's apparent that my fervour for this project was born from a profound sense of purpose. I yearned to initiate change, to extend aid to women in crises and to honour the shared dreams that had once ignited Halimah's and my excitement about future collaborative efforts. My lack of prior experience in business or product development was overshadowed by sheer determination and creativity, allowing me to persist. Every small stride I made brought me closer to my objective and further honed my skill of transforming my pain and affection for Halimah into a therapeutic force for good.

In crafting my inaugural business plan, I was able to pinpoint the central issues my venture would tackle, broadly encompassing three main themes: the stark deficiency of freely available menstrual products for women denied access or affordability; the toxic constituents of conventional menstrual products; and the significant environmental toll of these products. My primary objective was to create a business model enabling the provision of pads to women in dire straits, spanning from refugees in camps to the homeless dotting Britain's streets.

A chorus of voices – family, friends and business advisors – proposed that my focus should be directed towards establishing the business and cultivating profits prior to distributing free products for charitable causes. Nevertheless, I was unswerving in my conviction that supplying free menstrual pads to women grappling with poverty should be woven into the fabric of my business model from the outset. It was not to be deferred to a later stage as a mere emblem of corporate social responsibility.

The deeper I delved into the issues underpinning the limited access to and affordability of menstrual pads, the more this conviction cemented itself. I was steadfast – the ethos of kindness had to remain a cornerstone of my venture, or else I risked eroding the very foundation of my motivation, my purpose and the promise I had made to my Halimah.

As a result, my business model was imbued with a social mission. This decision felt right, transcending the realm of mere charity. It was an homage to Halimah's lofty aspirations, a pledge to leave a positive imprint on the lives of women and our shared environment. It was my pathway to contributing meaningfully to society while upholding the promise I had made to my daughter.

Where there is poverty, period poverty prevails

As I immersed myself more deeply in the issue of period poverty, I came to recognise that my initial obliviousness to the problem was far from an anomaly. Despite the fact I had personally faced moments of anxiety due to the scarcity of menstrual products, my investigation seemed to stir up more questions than it answered. The lack of readily available information was disheartening.

Having grown up with three sisters, I found the notion of periods being a taboo topic in our household peculiar. Although discussions about our menstrual cycles were expressly off-limits around our brothers or father, our parents surreptitiously maintained a specific cupboard stocked with pads, my mother vigilantly overseeing the supply to guarantee it was never empty.

A particular memory resurfaces of a time when my mother and older sister were away in Denmark, leaving my two younger sisters and me to navigate the household. As teenagers, we concocted a system to alert our father when our pad supply was dwindling. Exclamations such as, 'Oh no, there's only one left in the cupboard!' would echo across the house, ensuring our message reached his ears. Being an exceptional parent, he would ensure replenishment of the stock within the hour.

However, my experience was far from universal, and my research laid bare a multitude of circumstances wherein girls and women grappled with their period poverty in silence, both within the UK and overseas. When I initiated my investigation into these issues in 2011, the term 'period poverty' was yet to emerge. I thus referred to those ensnared in this predicament simply as women in crisis. The phrase 'period poverty' was eventually coined six years later in 2017 by the UK-based charity, Plan International, in a report titled 'Break the barriers: Girls' experiences of menstruation in the UK'.[4] The issue was then significantly amplified in the media landscape in 2018, amid the celebrity-driven #metoo movement.[5]

Despite the shroud of being taboo and the general lack of awareness, the reality remained stark and unignorable: countless girls and women globally lacked access to affordable, let alone complimentary menstrual products. This disparity often precipitated a host of devastating consequences, including missed school or work, infections and, in extreme instances, a descent into crime through stealing menstrual products or homelessness.

These pressing issues served as the compass that guided me to devise a business model capable of delivering pads to women in crisis, from the Syrian refugees I'd read about at Lahore airport to the homeless women huddled on Britain's pavements. While some advocated that I place profit generation ahead of philanthropy, I remained steadfast in my belief that generosity was to be the lifeblood of my business model.

In retrospect, I can pinpoint numerous occasions when I was caught without menstrual products and had to craft makeshift pads from folded toilet or kitchen paper. However, it never dawned on me that this was a pervasive problem. As girls and women, we're compelled by societal conditioning to internalise blame and manage with what's at hand. We are innately resourceful, but frequently fail to demand our rights, choosing silence over confrontation. Perhaps this reticence is a contributing factor to period poverty failing to command the attention it warrants. Even a century post women's suffrage, we are still navigating a labyrinth of hurdles to access basic essentials.

As I set to work on addressing period poverty, I could almost hear the disdainful voice of a highbrow male politician echoing in my mind: 'We've already granted women equal pay, abolished the tampon tax and we're even dispensing free menstrual products in schools; what more could they possibly demand, free products universally?' It was painfully apparent that certain individuals were unwilling to concede the gravity of the issue.

While empathising with the tribulations endured by women in refugee camps was intuitive, I found unearthing the magnitude of the problem in Britain to be a profound revelation. In 2011, though some articles reported on homeless women in the UK, concrete statistics centred specifically on this demographic were frustratingly scarce. This epiphany galvanised me to partner with homeless charities and women's refuge initiatives.

In 2022, Centrepoint, the charity for homeless youth in Britain, unveiled a report 'In Her Shoes', disclosing that upwards of 46,000 young women sought assistance from their local authorities due to homelessness or the looming threat thereof that year.[6] The report further underscored that domestic violence was the principal cause of homelessness for 15% of women aged between sixteen and twenty-four. In addition, these young women were subject to sexual assault, rape and the omnipresent dread of sexual exploitation while homeless. It was a heart-wrenching notion to think that many of these vulnerable young women, grappling with such monumental adversities, were also compelled to make agonising choices between purchasing food or menstrual products with the solitary pound gifted to them by a benevolent stranger on London's streets.

However, the need for access to menstrual products isn't confined to homeless women. The rising number of food banks in the UK indicates that all individuals grappling to afford food would likely encounter similar struggles in procuring menstrual products. There exists an undeniable correlation between financial poverty and period poverty.

My quest to identify women enduring period poverty led me through a veritable labyrinth. I discovered that by collaborating with organisations and groups focusing on various manifestations of poverty, I could pinpoint geographic epicentres of period poverty. For instance, government statistics on child poverty, predicated on areas denoted as indices of multiple deprivation, facilitated my identification of communities where women might find affording menstrual products challenging.

Just a few days prior to drafting this passage, I received a call on my period poverty hotline from a firefighter stationed in Greater Manchester. His mission was to inform low-income women that they could reach out to the fire service to have a free fire alarm installed. He shared with me the unsettling correlation between period poverty and an elevated likelihood of fires in the home. The reason? Women experiencing period poverty were frequently wrestling with other forms of suffering, including domestic violence, alcoholism and drug abuse.

He proposed that we embed messages in the packaging of menstrual products donated to food banks to help reach these women. In response, I conceived a campaign slogan dubbed 'Pants on Fire', which he loved. I've found that the most inventive and inspiring solutions often stem from collaborations with people operating in entirely different fields.

In terms of period poverty, I've grasped that it materialises wherever financial poverty persists. However, a revelation that took me by surprise is that a significant number of women relying on food banks are not unemployed, but rather employed in low-wage jobs. This issue, affecting millions of women in the UK, often slips under the radar. These women are in professional roles, including teaching and nursing; individuals who nurture us when we're ailing or educate our children are teetering on the brink of subsistence.

Reflecting on this, I find it unsettling that many of us have accepted makeshift pads as a commonplace solution to period poverty – primarily because women, known for our resilience, often manage without voicing our hardships. However, now we're aware of the grave global situation, it's high time we acknowledged the harsh reality that individuals being denied access to basic menstrual products is not just alarming, but utterly preposterous.

Period poverty in schools

Being a staunch advocate for increased period awareness and the crucial need for accessible menstrual products, I was driven to effect change not only within the UK, but also in less fortunate corners of the globe. Part of my strategy included donating menstrual products to schools in impoverished areas worldwide. At the same time, I recognised the critical need to combat period poverty within my local community. As a result, I set off on a quest to supply Derby schools with complimentary pads and to promote open discussions about menstruation.

Upon the arrival of my initial stock container, I promptly reached out to local schools. For those expressing interest in my complimentary pad donation, I took it upon myself to ensure they were perpetually supplied. Dishearteningly, some schools reported that period poverty wasn't an issue as girls never requested products. This feedback underscored the need for a different approach with these schools; if the topic was taboo, then undoubtedly, the girls within these institutions were suffering silently.

Plan International, a charity that promotes children's rights and equality for girls, reported distressing statistics in 2017: 48% of girls aged between fourteen and twenty-one in the UK felt embarrassed by their periods.[7] In addition, the report indicated that 14% of girls were unaware of what was occurring when they had their first period, while 26% didn't know how to manage it. More alarming was the fact that 78% of girls felt uneasy discussing their periods with their teachers. The repercussions of this deficient education and awareness are multifaceted, leading to feelings of shame, embarrassment and even school absences.

In March 2018, I, along with a small team of trustees, launched the Gift Wellness Foundation, marking a pivotal moment in our quest to impact the Derby community positively. We hosted a Period Poverty Forum, inviting all local schools and women's organisations to foster awareness and promote education about periods. It was during this forum that we saw progress with schools that had previously dismissed period poverty. I like to think that, in part due to our efforts, Derby became the UK's first city to eradicate period poverty in schools. We'll explore the aftermath of our Period Poverty Forum more comprehensively in Chapter 4.

Working with international schools presented more complexities, barring the Halimah School of Excellence in Pakistan, for which I transferred funds from The Halimah Trust to fulfil the girls' needs.

Locally sourced menstrual pads for the school's 450 girls proved to be a more cost-efficient and environmentally friendly solution than shipping Gift Wellness anion pads (more detail on anions later in this chapter). This approach also supported the local economy. Concurrently, I sought a natural menstrual products manufacturer in Pakistan.

Numerous charities reached out to the Gift Wellness Foundation, gathering aid to deliver to schools, women's projects and institutions like women's hospitals and prisons in Africa, India and the Middle East. An international aid charity would collect products from us, incorporate them into their aid container and dispatch it to the corresponding port within weeks. They then shared photos, sometimes videos, of our products being distributed. It was, and still is, overwhelmingly emotional and profoundly moving to witness the images of women in crisis situations, standing outside their tents, clutching a box of our Gift pads in war-ravaged locations like Aleppo. The most impactful images featured women carrying children or holding a child's hand, their bare feet etched in my memory.

It wasn't conventional business triumphs, such as securing the contract with a major high-street chain, winning awards or media features, that signified accomplishment for me. These deeply human moments reminded me of the purpose I was fulfilling, the promise I had kept to Halimah. The faces of the women and girls in those photos bore a resemblance to her spirit.

Regrettably, there remain, and I fear always will, countless women and girls we can't reach. For instance, girls in parts of South Asia and Africa are denied education upon reaching puberty and are subsequently married off for the economic benefit of their families. Charities like UNICEF, Oxfam and Save the Children tirelessly strive to address these issues, but substantial change necessitates governmental intervention. While Pakistan, under Imran Khan's administration, passed an anti-dowry law in 2020, the effective enforcement of this regulation remains challenging in remote villages where traditional patriarchal systems still prevail.

Upholding dignity

As our world contends with an alarming 100 million people forcibly displaced due to political, social and cultural turmoil, the plight of women and girls among these refugees is profoundly distressing. The United Nations High Commission for Refugees reports that over half of these displaced individuals are women and girls who often endure dire circumstances.[8] For many, the lack of fundamental necessities, including approximately 12 million without access to basic sanitary protection, is a harsh daily reality. They resort to makeshift pads torn from their clothing, sacrificing their dignity and risking infection.

In collaboration with charities operating within refugee camps, we endeavour to uphold these women's dignity by directly supplying menstrual pads. Yet, the lack of sanitary protection is merely one facet of the broader issues plaguing women in refugee camps. Alongside this, they confront marginalisation, sexual and gender-based violence, child marriage and, in some instances, kidnapping, trafficking or forced marriages. Their displacement extends beyond the physical into the emotional and social realms, leaving them bereft of community and a sense of belonging.

The Covid-19 pandemic further exacerbated their hardships. Because women and girls were trapped with their abusers, domestic abuse incidents surged. Additionally, the pandemic posed logistical challenges to organisations and charities aiming to aid refugee women, compounding their struggles.

In countries like Syria, where women had made strides towards gender equality, the effects of displacement and disease rolled back their progress. The Ukrainian conflict amplified these difficulties, with increasing reports of rape and sexual abuse among internally displaced women. The trauma of war and displacement yields lasting physical and emotional wounds.

It is crucial to recognise that many of these refugee women are their families' primary caregivers. This burden adds layers of complexity to their access to aid and support. They form the backbone of their communities, yet frequently grapple alone without the requisite support and resources to care for themselves and their loved ones.

Evidently, urgent action is required to assist women refugees in these challenging times. Economic opportunities for women refugees could help alleviate poverty, bolster gender equality and foster inclusive work, all while aiding local and global economies. It is equally important to ensure women's voices and needs are included in policies and programmes created to protect them. This inclusion can be accomplished through education and training opportunities, empowering them to achieve self-sufficiency and support their families.

However, the cornerstone of this multifaceted approach, and arguably the most formidable hurdle to surmount, lies in altering societal attitudes towards acknowledging and respecting women's rights and safeguarding their dignity. Without this fundamental shift, the prospect of meaningful long-term change remains a distant dream.

As we tackle the ongoing refugee crisis, it is vital to note the distinct struggles and lived experiences of women in refugee settings. Women and girls make up more than half of the 100 million people globally who are forcibly displaced, underscoring our responsibility to step forward and aid these individuals in their time of utmost need.

In Chapter 4, I draw from my personal experiences during a deployment to Lebanon where I was involved in distributing menstrual products in Syrian refugee camps. This visceral exposure to realities on the ground reinforced for me the urgency and necessity of striving towards a world in which refugee women are afforded the dignity, respect and assistance to enable them to reconstruct their shattered lives. Crucially, this transformation needs to be embedded in a larger societal paradigm shift, recognising women's rights and dignity as fundamental. Until such a change in attitudes is achieved, sustainable progress will remain elusive.

The menace of toxic menstrual products

My research unveiled the unsettling reality of toxic constituents found in menstrual products widely sold in high-street stores across the UK. Astonishingly, these essentials of every woman's life are frequently made from inferior materials that not only adversely affect women's health, but also amplify discomfort during menstruation.

A recent guest blog for the Women's Environmental Network by the CHEM Trust shed light on the potential perils of using conventional menstrual products.[9] The blog disclosed the alarming presence of harmful chemicals such as bisphenols, pesticides, volatile organic compounds and phthalates in many of these products. Particularly concerning are phthalates, a class of chemicals utilised to enhance plastic durability, which are recognised carcinogens and can inflict harm on human reproductive, neurological and developmental systems.

This insight from the CHEM Trust underpins the necessity of adopting safe and sustainable menstrual products for the dual benefit of our health and our planet. An article by Andrea Chisholm MD in Verywell Health,[10] along with a study conducted by the University of La Plata in Argentina,[11] highlighted that a staggering 85% of tampons and pads contain glyphosate. This known carcinogen, widely used as a pesticide in the infamous weed killer brand Roundup, has been linked to an elevated risk of cancer, particularly breast and uterine cancers.

Further compounding the issue, numerous menstrual products incorporate potentially harmful fragrances, which could provoke skin irritation and allergic reactions. Such chemicals could give rise to a myriad of health problems, including skin afflictions, reproductive complications, endometriosis, infertility and even cancer.

Beyond the physical and mental-health repercussions, toxic menstrual products inflict a profound impact on women's day-to-day lives. Utilising products made with inferior and harmful ingredients can lead to a spectrum of distressing symptoms, impairing women's ability to concentrate and perform optimally at school or work. This impairment could precipitate setbacks in educational attainment and career progression, ultimately inhibiting women from actualising their full potential.

Thus, it's critical that we prioritise the promotion and development of safe, sustainable menstrual products. Not only would this reduce the harmful impacts on women's health and their daily lives, but it would also align with broader environmental sustainability goals. The responsibility to facilitate this lies not only with manufacturers and regulators, but also with us as informed consumers who can effect change through our purchasing choices.

With a resolute commitment to instigate change, I established Gift pads, a line of menstrual products designed with the conscious intention of enhancing women's health and wellbeing, while also fostering responsible environmental stewardship. Crafted from safe, natural ingredients, Gift pads are gentle on women's bodies, pose no harm to young girls and demonstrate eco-friendly characteristics. The brand's charitable ethos underscores its devotion to minimising environmental impact and its commitment to using sustainable materials whenever feasible.

My aspiration was to conceive a product that not only advocates for women's health and planetary sustainability, but also extends assistance to those who find menstrual products inaccessible or unaffordable. For every pack of Gift pads sold, the brand donates pads to women in crisis, thereby empowering them to reclaim control over their menstrual health and equipping them with the necessary tools to unlock their full potential.

The provision of safe, reliable menstrual products is a non-negotiable human right. My customers can rest assured, knowing that Gift pads are devoid of harmful chemicals capable of inducing illness and potential carcinogenic effects. I stand firm in my commitment to ensure universal access to safe and sustainable menstrual products, with Gift Wellness being a testament to the conviction that every woman deserves to experience comfort during her menstrual cycle.

The transformative power of tourmaline

As I set sail on my venture to found a business that would not just provide a crucial product, but also extend support to women in crisis, I was aware that I needed a truly unique factor to differentiate my brand in the saturated menstrual-product market. This led to my discovery of tourmaline, a semi-precious mineral that would not only become a hallmark of my brand, but also significantly alter the trajectory of my life.

My fortuitous encounter with tourmaline occurred in 2011, during my pilgrimage to Pakistan with my husband, mother and sister for the inauguration of the Halimah School of Excellence. We arrived a few days prior to the big event, so we capitalised on our time by visiting relatives dotted across various regions of the Punjab. During one such visit, we found ourselves navigating the vibrant streets of Gujar Khan. Serendipitously, my mother, Noor Safia, and I discovered a hidden treasure – a charming little store discreetly tucked away from the crowded main street. As we stepped inside, we were enveloped by the calming fragrance of herbs and welcomed by the soft chime of a doorbell.

It was here that we met an enigmatic Chinese herbalist whose sage-like presence instantly held our fascination. Dressed in a crisp white doctor's coat, he emerged and greeted us warmly. With rapt attention, he listened as my mother discussed her concerns about her elevated blood pressure.

Following a pulse check and some enquiries, he introduced us to a wide canvas belt embedded with tourmaline. He explained that this mineral was known for regulating body temperature, enhancing circulation, balancing hormones and alleviating fatigue. Eager to explore this remedy, my mother wrapped the belt around her waist, instantly feeling a sense of relief. Whether influenced by a placebo effect or guided by a woman's intuition, she decided to give it a try.

As we expressed our gratitude and prepared to depart, the herbalist spoke to his female colleague in Mandarin and gestured towards me. This prompted her to return with a sample pack of anion 'lady napkins':

menstrual pads made with the same tourmaline-infused material. He clarified that an Indian company, Winalite International, had pioneered this material for menstrual products and he offered me a few samples to trial.

There was something particularly extraordinary about this chance meeting, prompting me to coax the shopkeeper into selling me a couple of packs. Unbeknown to me then, this marked the inception of my journey to bring the benefits of tourmaline to women worldwide through my brand, Gift.

As I anticipated the chance to test out the intriguing new pads the Chinese herbalist had given me, a wave of hope washed over me. For as long as memory served, I had trudged through my menstrual cycles armed only with conventional supermarket pads. Now, however, I possessed a hint of something that could potentially transform that experience.

Three weeks later, the moment finally arrived. Back on British soil, I cautiously unwrapped the foil packaging and the plastic cover of the pad, revealing a surprisingly modest-looking item. It was slim, slightly coarse and quite basic in design, but the pale green layer situated just beneath the thin top sheet immediately drew my attention. I knew this was the tourmaline.

Upon testing the product, I instantly observed a change. The customary fatigue and discomfort

I usually experienced by day three of my period were conspicuously absent. It was astounding. This serendipitous discovery dovetailed perfectly with my evolving business plan, convincing me that I needed to delve deeper into it.

I contacted the Indian company and ordered more sample packs, which I distributed among a dozen friends and relatives for their feedback. To my delight, they too reported positive effects, mirroring my own experience. However, as I envisioned myself marketing these pads, I felt the design and materials the company used were too basic and, crucially, the packaging of the pads was not sufficiently eco-friendly. It dawned on me then that my mission wasn't just to introduce this potent mineral to women through a superior quality pad, but also to ensure that this was done in an environmentally considerate manner.

A personal bond with tourmaline

Six years had elapsed since my initial discovery of tourmaline's potent properties in a humble shop halfway across the world, and my unique Gift pads were capturing the attention of women all over Britain. It was during this period that my comprehension of tourmaline deepened, fuelling my passion to disseminate the benefits of this semi-precious mineral to women worldwide. Little had I anticipated how profoundly the encounter with the enigmatic Chinese herbalist would transform my life trajectory, nor how seamlessly it would dovetail with my personal passions and convictions.

In 2017, at the Allergy & Free From Show in London, an unexpected interaction with a naturopath unveiled yet another intriguing piece of the puzzle: tourmaline is one of the two birthstones associated with October, my birth month (the other being opal). This personal connection further amplified my appreciation for this potent mineral.

Tourmaline mineral

Throughout the annals of history, I discovered that tourmaline gems have been cherished for their stunning beauty and their purported ability to invigorate the mind, body and spirit. It was said that the diverse range of colours, hues and shades embedded within the stones is unrivalled, fuelling the belief in their capacity to kindle creativity and artistic expression. As an artist and writer, I found myself drawn to this narrative, sensing a deep resonance with the mineral.

As well as this personal affinity that pulled me towards tourmaline, there was also an association with my mission. Within spiritual circles, the stone is traditionally associated with the zodiac sign of Libra, often symbolised by the scales of justice. This symbol underscores tourmaline's balancing properties, believed to instil strength and tranquillity in its possessor or wearer. As someone who experienced the tempestuous symptoms of pre-menstrual stress (PMS), I felt an intimate alignment with this mineral and its journey. Its purported ability to harmonise hormones, alleviate tension and restore a peaceful equilibrium between mind, body and soul positioned tourmaline as an ideal companion for menstruating women.

Fuelled by my conviction, I embarked on a mission: to bring the virtues of this mineral to as many women as possible in a manner that benefited their health and preserved the environment. Immersing myself further in the world of tourmaline, I was struck again by a sense of serendipity. The lore of ancient mystics and the correlation with my own birthstone only deepened the allure of this powerful mineral. However, my passion to incorporate tourmaline into my products was not based solely on tales and legends.

Unlocking the power of tourmaline

In the time between my fortuitous encounter with the Chinese doctor in Pakistan and the crafting of my first business plan, I plunged into extensive research about the scientifically proven advantages and applications of tourmaline, particularly regarding women's menstrual health. This research revealed disturbing trends, including an alarming rise in menstrual-health issues, infertility and chronic diseases among women. The staggering evidence of harmful ingredients in many mainstream menstrual products only affirmed my suspicion of a connection between declining women's health and toxic products.

The wealth of knowledge I uncovered, documented in esteemed publications from Harvard, the National Library of Medicine and various scientific and medical journals worldwide, was nothing short of astounding.[12] Tourmaline's ability to balance hormones, ease PMS symptoms, enhance circulation and regulate body temperature became abundantly clear.

Motivated by the compelling scientific evidence and a deep sense of responsibility, I was driven to share the potency of this mineral with as many women as possible. It was this dedication to research and evidence-based practice that helped differentiate my brand from other products.[13]

Tourmaline, defined as a 'boron silicate' by scientists,[14] possesses profound purifying qualities that render it anything but boring or silly. This multifaceted mineral, teeming with anions, not only bolsters the immune system, but also enriches our lives in a myriad of subtle ways, frequently unbeknown to us. It has been, and continues to be, an integral component of various sectors, such as healthcare and environmental conservation, its presence often concealed in plain sight within our own homes, silently contributing to our wellbeing.

Tourmaline, especially in its pulverised form, pervades our everyday existence. It can be found in many hair products, refrigerators, air purifiers, water filters and even showerheads. However, its influence is not restricted to domestic arenas. In the agricultural realm, it functions as a greenhouse air purifier and a growth stimulant for plants. The medical field recognises and utilises its analgesic and anti-inflammatory properties, but what truly distinguishes tourmaline is its unparalleled capacity to produce negative ions, effectively neutralising harmful positive ions in our environment. Hence, it acts as an essential tool in air revitalisation and purification.

Although tourmaline is indeed aesthetically pleasing, its numerous health benefits far transcend its visual allure, rendering it an invaluable tool for enhancing our daily existence. As a dominantly right-brain individual, I initially grappled with comprehending the scientific intricacies of tourmaline and its mechanisms, but as my research intensified, I began unravelling the true magic of this mineral. Millennia of solar absorption have endowed tourmaline with an extraordinary magnetic property, initiated by the application of energy or pressure – a phenomenon known as the pyroelectric effect.

In layman's terms, when tourmaline is subjected to pressure or heat, for example when it's embedded in our menstrual pads and pressed against our body, it becomes ionised, generating negative ions. These negative ions, also known as anions, are minute particles bearing an extra electron. They bind with positively charged particles in their vicinity, including bacteria, free radicals, allergens and pollutants. Thus, they amalgamate to form dense particles, too heavy to remain airborne, which then descend to the ground. These particles are absorbed into the pad, hence shielding the body from their potential harm.

Negative ions are not exclusive to tourmaline. They abound in nature – in ocean waves, rustling tree leaves and thunderstorms. These natural phenomena saturate the environment with anions, which are reminiscent of a brisk walk in the park on a windy day or the energy we feel from the crashing of waves on a sea shore, revitalising us when we are feeling low.

In addition to tourmaline's remarkable capacity to generate negative ions, it also emits far-infrared rays

(FIRs), a form of energy invisible to the human eye. FIRs can penetrate all layers of the human body, producing heat via a continuous self-electrifying charge. They permeate the body's deepest regions – bones, tissues and muscles – and gently expand the capillaries carrying blood. The resultant increased flow enhances blood oxygenation and regeneration, thereby deeply detoxifying the body, dissolving latent toxins and bolstering the function of major organs.

The extraordinary properties of tourmaline have been extensively scrutinised and corroborated by scientific research. A paper published by the University of Science and Technology Beijing stipulated that tourmaline continuously and spontaneously generates electrodes, displaying a potent capacity for absorbing heavy metals and other impurities.[15] Moreover, the FIRs emitted by tourmaline can effectively curtail the proliferation of bacteria within its immediate environment. This versatility accords tourmaline with potential applications in diverse fields, from water decontamination to air-pollution filtration.

The salubrious impact of tourmaline on the nervous system, coupled with the improved efficiency of the organs and tissues, renders it a unique and potent mineral. Its pairing of negative ions and FIRs positions tourmaline as an esteemed yet under-appreciated player in the realm of health and wellness. Admittedly, at the start of my product development journey, my strategy was based more on theory than belief, but

I regarded the incorporation of tourmaline into my menstrual pads as an innovative method of harnessing its benefits to improve women's overall wellbeing.

I soon discovered that when it's integrated into menstrual pads, tourmaline's properties are particularly advantageous. They aid in mitigating and preventing infections and unpleasant odours resulting from bacterial activity. Tourmaline also helps sustain a healthy pH balance, regulate menstrual cycles and induce a general sense of tranquillity.

From the customer testimonials at Gift Wellness, it's clear that tourmaline-infused pads are truly transforming women's menstrual experiences.[16] The reviews tell a heartening story of improved skin condition, reduced irritation, alleviation of pain and enhanced sleep quality. Many customers share how they generally feel better during their menstrual cycle after switching to Gift pads. Such positive experiences often lead them to set up a monthly subscription, ensuring they're consistently equipped with Gift products.

An owner of a natural health store in Derbyshire relayed a particularly inspiring account about his customers who have daughters. Several have reported that since they started using Gift pads, their daughters are experiencing fewer disruptive menstrual symptoms, leading to less absenteeism from school due to period-related issues.

Ethical and legal considerations of using tourmaline

When I first learned about the company that patented the tourmaline anion layer specifically designed for menstrual pads, I was intrigued by the promise of its potential to improve women's health. However, I wasn't content to take the company's word for it, so I buckled down, pouring months into dissecting the world of tourmaline, understanding it and probing it from a business perspective. What I found left me perplexed. The scientific evidence supporting the benefits of tourmaline was substantial, but it was tinged with a frustration that was hard to shake off.

The world of commercialisation isn't as straightforward as we'd all like it to be. The hefty costs associated with conducting clinical trials mean that an entrepreneur like me, dabbling in tourmaline, can't explicitly claim the mineral's medical benefits. The best I can do is skirt around the edges, implying, hinting at the benefits, but never outright stating them. This dance of ambiguity, bookended with a tedious medical disclaimer, is a considerable stumbling block, a hurdle that has me gritting my teeth in frustration. Mark my words, though; the moment one of the big brands wakes up to the immense potential of this wonder mineral, they'll be waving around a medical device licence faster than you can say PMS!

When it comes to sourcing tourmaline, there is a host of countries to choose from, including Russia, the USA, Burma, Brazil, Mozambique and China. However, as is the case with all mining industries, it comes with its share of problems, one of the gravest being the horrifying reports of child labour.[17] I have to be meticulous, scrutinising my choice of manufacturer to ensure every component, every ounce of material I use, is ethically sourced.

Through all this, one question keeps nagging at me, gnawing at the corners of my mind. Why are tourmaline-infused products not available in various forms on the National Health Service (NHS)? Are they being edged out, eclipsed by the colossal pharmaceutical corporations and conglomerates that manufacture the most widely and cheaply available menstrual products? Is there some sort of underhand blocking at play? Regardless of the murky reasons, one thing is clear: I must shine a spotlight on the alternative to the pads we have 'always' used – an alternative that goes beyond mere hygiene and proactively bolsters women's health.

Reflecting on my decision to incorporate tourmaline into Gift's menstrual pads, I feel a profound sense of pride. I am honoured to have offered women a healthier and more sustainable alternative for managing their menstrual cycle. It extends beyond merely supplying a product – it represents a move towards empowerment and choice. The overwhelmingly positive feedback from thousands of satisfied customers confirms my decision to utilise tourmaline. As my brand continues to innovate and enhance its products, I remain committed to providing women with the highest standard of menstrual care.

THREE

Bringing Gift Wellness
To Market

'When someone is counting out gold for you, don't look at your hands, or the gold. Look at the giver.'
— Rumi[18]

As my product development journey progressed, I knew that I wanted to turn my vision into a successful business that could truly make a difference. This chapter is about my business development, from the inception of the Gift brand name to the arrival of the first container of products in January 2013. I share how I built my business purpose and created prototype products, which underwent extensive testing to ensure that they were safe and effective. I take you through the process of setting up Gift Wellness Ltd, including the challenges of bootstrapping and the importance of visualising the end goal.

Later in the chapter, I share my approach to the market, from working with independent stores to distributors for major high-street chains. I explore the pros and cons of selling business-to-business (B2B) versus business-to-consumer (B2C) and discuss other avenues, such as Amazon, that I pursued to expand my reach. I also discuss the changing face of marketing and how I had to adapt to the new realities of the marketplace.

This chapter is about taking an idea and turning it into a successful business, and the challenges and rewards that come with that journey. It's about finding the courage to pursue your dreams and the determination to make them a reality.

Birth of a brand: Gift®

One of my younger sisters, Saiqa, joined me at my kitchen table as we spread out a constellation of notes and doodles, our first go at potential brand names and designs. My siblings and I are blessed with a vein of creativity, a gift we inherited from our mother. As a skilled designer, Saiqa was the perfect confidante to bounce ideas off of in my search for a fitting brand name for my product.

We busied ourselves, our pens dancing across the paper, jotting down names and phrases that encapsulated the essence of the business. Words such as 'ethical', 'natural', 'anion' and 'wellbeing' surfaced and mingled, creating a mosaic of potential identities.

It was during a discussion on the philanthropic cornerstone of the business, and its implications for me as well as the intended beneficiaries, that I exclaimed, 'It's a gift!' Saiqa and I locked eyes, our thoughts aligning in the unspoken understanding that only siblings can share.

'That's it, Gift,' Saiqa announced. After volleying the name back and forth, occasionally testing variations like 'Gifted' or 'The Gift', we found ourselves gravitating back to the original. Thus, we elected Gift as our choice. It encapsulates the concept of a gift for women who benefit from my products, a gift for those who receive them through donation, a gift to the environment and, indeed, a gift in the form of a tribute to my Halimah, whose dream it was to establish an ethical enterprise that would bring prosperity to all it touched.

Once I'd decided on Gift as the name for my product line, the next task was to determine a name for the company. Adding 'Wellness' felt appropriate, and I promptly registered the name with Companies House. Although the online registration process was straightforward, I had to look up the definitions of different company types and share structures. Nonetheless, on 11 June 2012, Gift Wellness Limited was officially brought into existence.

A few days later, I formulated the strapline 'because you deserve it' for the Gift brand. I hold a staunch belief that women deserve only the finest quality products, especially when it concerns the most delicate and intimate parts of their bodies. The brand registration was somewhat convoluted, but with the guidance of a kind gentleman from the Intellectual Property Office (IPO), I successfully navigated the regulations and submitted my application. As per his advice, I initially used the ™ symbol and transitioned to ® once the registration received approval.

With the company structure in place, I was in a position to open a bank account and engage with a business account manager. I opted to apply for a loan to cover the manufacturing and shipping costs of my initial inventory. To support this, the bank required a projected profit and loss statement for the upcoming three years and a comprehensive business plan, covering aspects from potential risks and competitors to marketing and sales strategies.

The financial aspect of this venture posed quite the challenge, but, as is his custom, my husband Ash stepped in to lend a hand. Ash, a name signifying 'longing' in Persian, launched his career as a mechanical engineer, precision-engineering jet engines. He became my left brain, my mathematical cornerstone whenever Excel and calculations came into play.

I marvelled as he meticulously constructed a comprehensive spreadsheet, outlining all the costs associated with the various business elements. He subsequently introduced formulas into each column, forecasting the costs and sales, profits and losses. I printed the resulting document, a testament to his diligence, and presented it to the bank manager in a sleek folder alongside my business plan.

A few days later, I was thrilled to receive the news: I had secured my initial loan of £25,000. These funds would propel the launch of my enterprise and pave the way for my dream of an ethical business to materialise.

Even before finalising my manufacturing partner, I had a lucid vision for my product packaging. It needed to be aesthetically pleasing, mirroring the essence of my brand name Gift, but also readily identifiable as a pack of menstrual pads. As an artist, I was driven by the idea of creating a package that was stylish enough to be displayed in bathrooms or on work desks without invoking discomfort. I was determined to dismantle the notion that menstrual pads are an item to be concealed and stigmatised. In my view, this change would simplify the process for men buying these essential items for the women in their lives, removing any hesitation or embarrassment.

My perspective on this matter has evolved over the years. Now, I put greater emphasis on the normalisation of menstruation and the inclusion of men in discussions about this natural life process. There's no reason for feelings of shame or embarrassment. It is my firm belief that we should unreservedly expect men to acknowledge this fact of life and participate in conversations about it without any unease. This shift in perspective has influenced my brand's mission, steering it towards debunking the stigma surrounding menstruation while ensuring menstrual-care products are accessible to all.

Product research and development

Throughout the developmental stages of my business, I engaged in ceaseless communication with potential manufacturers for my Gift pads. My main channels of contact were Skype and phone calls, as neither Zoom nor WhatsApp were available in those days, but Skype didn't always prove reliable. I encountered numerous vexing meetings in which the video failed and the audio quality was poor, compounded by a language barrier with the manufacturers speaking English with a thick Chinese accent. This made comprehension challenging.

Fortunately, a friend residing in Shenzhen was able to personally visit the factory of the manufacturer I was considering, a step that affirmed their credibility. Nonetheless, a sense of unease and risk persisted, even with the extent of due diligence and research conducted. It felt akin to taking a leap of faith, a necessary courage when bootstrapping a fresh business venture, requiring both nerves of steel and unwavering faith in one's instincts.

For further assurance, I relied on Kissie Li, my Chinese account manager, to guide me through the factory floor where products similar to mine were being crafted. This afforded me an in-depth understanding of the manufacturing process, the working conditions and the quality of the manufacturer's output. Ensuring that the products were being crafted in an ethical and sustainable fashion was paramount to me.

As I navigated my business's development, building trust and fostering relationships with suppliers emerged as key factors in my brand's success. I continue to visit the factories, meet the workers and ascertain that they are paid fairly. It is critical to ensure that my personal and business values are echoed by every participant in the process.

Over the course of approximately twelve months, I painstakingly crafted the recipe for my Gift pads. I was resolute in my aim to produce a product that would offer the utmost comfort and protection for menstruating women, without sacrificing style or quality. To attain this, I began by ordering hundreds of material samples for the pad's construction, which would consist of no fewer than nine layers. I invested countless hours into researching and testing these different materials, ensuring that each layer fulfilled a specific function and contributed to the product's overall efficacy.

Five layers of air-laid chlorine-free paper endows the pads with structure, ensuring they remain in place. The super absorbent middle layer is crucial for menstrual fluid absorption, while the benefits of the tourmaline layer include regulating the menstrual cycle, reducing the risk of infection and balancing hormones. The super soft and perforated top sheet makes the pads comfortable to wear and protects against skin irritation. The bottom layer was initially plastic, but in my commitment to ecological sustainability, I have transitioned to a corn-starch-based alternative.

Once the first prototype samples were assembled, I circulated them among a select group of friends and family who I trusted to provide honest feedback. After several rounds of prototyping and testing, I fine-tuned the materials and shapes of the pads to optimise their effectiveness and comfort. As my testers began to experience the pads' positive impact on their menstrual cycles, interest in the product grew and enquiries about its availability for purchase ensued.

After three rounds of prototyping and testing, I was finally content with the material composition and ready to green light my chosen manufacturer to procure the necessary ingredients, assemble the pads and prepare my first twenty-foot container of stock. The journey had been long and arduous, but I took immense pride in the product I had shaped and was eager to introduce it to the world.

While I eagerly awaited the arrival of my raw materials, I immersed myself in designing the packaging for my new range of Gift menstrual products. I drafted designs for my normal pads, long pads and daily pantyliners. Once I'd decided on the quantity of pads for each pack, Kissie forwarded the packaging template.

I enlisted a local design agency to transform my sketches into print-ready artwork. The same agency had created and developed my initial Gift Wellness website. Although the price was steep, I was certain the investment would pay dividends.

The day finally arrived when the Gift brand was officially birthed into the world. From the moment I held the finished product in my hands, I knew it was more than just a menstrual pad; it was a symbol of empowerment, care and positive change. The packaging exuded positivity, with a vibrant and welcoming design that spoke of the brand's underlying values. The aura that the Gift brand radiated was one of integrity, quality and commitment to making a genuine difference.

My heart swelled with pride and fulfilment, for in my hands I held not just a product, but a beacon of hope and wellness for women. I was profoundly pleased with the Gift brand, and I felt that every ounce of effort had been worth it as I had created something that would touch the lives of countless women in a beautiful and meaningful way.

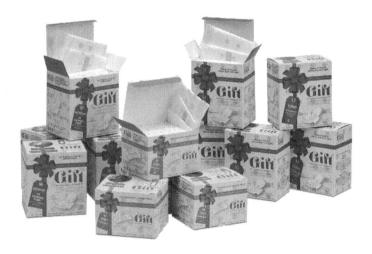

Gift pads product range

This was before the advent of platforms such as Fiverr and Upwork, which would have spared me a substantial amount of work. These days, Fiverr.com is my go-to resource for most needs and I consistently endorse it to nascent business owners. With Fiverr, establishing a professional, high-quality business costs a fraction of what it would have a few years ago.

What I find particularly appealing about platforms like Fiverr is their ability to connect me with skilled individuals globally. Many of these individuals hail from less privileged backgrounds, making the platform a levelling force in business opportunities irrespective of a person's origins. The range and calibre of talent available on these platforms is exemplary, and the rating system ensures I'm always collaborating with top-tier professionals. My current team includes a web developer in Pakistan, a Google Ads specialist from Sri Lanka, a copywriter from South Africa and a graphic designer from Bangladesh.

From first shipment to humanitarian aid

Ordering the ingredients and filling a twenty-foot container with stock took roughly ten weeks to accomplish. Afterwards, I had to endure another four weeks for the container to reach Felixstowe port, where it underwent scanning and processing. It nearly missed the pre-Christmas delivery window due to some eleventh-hour modifications to the design of the individual wrappers for each pad. Thankfully, I just managed to prevent a situation where my container would have languished at the port over the Christmas period, a delay which would have resulted in additional holding charges.

Finally, my inaugural container arrived just before Christmas 2012 at my storage facility in Walsall, owned by Midlands Toiletries. The proprietors, the Siddique brothers, were tremendously supportive. Farooq, the elder brother, took me under his wing, imparting a wealth of knowledge about importing and working with distributors. His kindness and magnanimity will always resonate with me, and I will forever appreciate the assistance he provided as I worked to get my fledgling enterprise up and running.

In the weeks prior, I had been formulating a sales strategy. However, before I could begin selling my products, an important matter demanded my attention.

During the Christmas holidays, my sister-in-law Nahida informed me about a local charity organisation that was collecting clothes, food and other essentials to fill an aid container set to be shipped to a Syrian refugee camp in January. I requested the organiser's contact information and dialled him up to ask if he could dispatch a van to gather as much of my stock as possible. Upon enquiring about the container's destination, I was staggered to discover it was heading to the Za'atari Syrian refugee camp – the very same camp I had read about in the airport magazine twenty months prior. The prospect of providing aid to the women I had seen in that article moved me to tears. Overwhelmed with emotion, I again envisioned myself delivering products to them.

When I asked the charity organiser if he could dispatch a van to retrieve a few pallets of menstrual pads, to my astonishment and dismay, he replied, 'Oh, sister, this container is being filled with vital things like food, clothing and medicine. We'll try to take some of your products next time.' I enquired where the charity was located, drove there and asked to meet with him. Struggling to suppress the anger, hurt and bewilderment welling within me, apart from the tear I could feel brimming in my eye, I asked him to imagine if his mother, sister, daughter or wife were displaced and living as a refugee... and no matter what happened, she was going to get her periods.

You can imagine his face... the woman in the headscarf had just said the 'p' word! I strove to ignore the numerous heads swivelling my way and emphasised that those women in the refugee camp were also someone's mother, daughter or sister.

He actually began to weep and confessed, 'I can't believe we overlooked such an important aspect of emergency aid.' Naturally, he dispatched a sizeable truck to my warehouse, loaded it with several pallets of stock and included them in the aid container. From that day forward, the charity organisation has continued to gather my menstrual pads for distribution to refugee camps.

While I took solace in my persistence paying off, my encounter with the charity organisation underscored the complexities embedded in donating products for emergency aid. It dawned on me that I would have to initiate numerous discussions with aid agencies, persuading them to appreciate menstrual products not as a non-essential luxury, but as an indispensable need.

From that moment, I've held hundreds of dialogues with various charity workers, and slowly but surely, my endeavours are beginning to bear fruit. Menstrual products are now increasingly being acknowledged as a critical element of emergency aid, rather than a discretionary add-on. Consequently, I hold a hopeful vision that more aid organisations will incorporate menstrual products in their packages, leading to enhanced health and wellbeing for innumerable women and girls in crisis situations.

Zareen preparing Syria shipment

Syrian refugee woman with Gift pads
in front of tent – Aleppo

Gift's strategic market entry and expansion

The Za'atari camp donation afforded me a head start in fulfilling my principal objective of donating pads to women in crisis for each pack Gift Wellness sold. However, my overarching ambition was to propel Gift into the retail mainstream, ideally landing its products on the shelves of prominent high-street chains. Being pragmatic, I recognised that breaking into such a prominent retailer would be no small feat, especially without a proven sales track record. To circumvent this challenge, I devised a tactical plan to build credibility through a ground-up strategy by reverse-engineering my approach to larger retailers' buyers.

Leveraging insights gleaned through conversations with Farooq and other industry insiders, I realised that high-street chains would be more amenable if other distributors and retailers were already on board. With this in mind, I initially approached various distributors who supplied stock to independent health stores. They, in turn, confirmed that they required evidence of demand, necessitating that I secure the interest and sales from a smattering of independent retailers.

This was uncharted territory for me. As sales are not my forte, persuading retailers to stock my products presented a novel challenge for me to vanquish. Determined, I resolved to personally reach out to independent retailers within my region of Derbyshire.

My maiden voyage led me to Natural Choice, an endearing shop owned by two brothers, Steve and Roy, nestled in Ashbourne, a charming market town in the heart of the Derbyshire Dales. I spoke with Steve, who is generous and was instantly captivated by my pads and mission to donate to women in crisis. This led to my first sale – a case of each of Gift's product lines, totalling seventy-two units. Steve's enthusiasm and faith were an inaugural victory, and he remains a cherished figure in my journey.

Buoyed by this initial success, I persisted in nurturing relationships with independent retailers and distributors, methodically expanding Gift's network. Within a month, I had rounded up around twelve independent retailers, and this fortified my confidence to pursue the distributor that was my real prize – The Health Store, located in Nottingham.

A buyer at The Health Store, a tall, slim man with a kind countenance, was impressed by how swiftly independent retailers were embracing Gift pads and commended my decision to participate in the prestigious Natural Products Europe trade show at London's Olympia. The buyer advocated for Gift's listing, though he asked that I channel retailer orders through The Health Store rather than Gift Wellness.

Our conversation took an unexpected turn when I alluded to my aspiration to be stocked in a multinational high-street health-food chain. His expression soured as he sternly advised against mentioning it to independent retailers, who harboured a strong disdain for the high-street giant.

This interaction underscored the importance of understanding and resonating with The Health Store's clientele. These independent retailers – typically small family-run businesses or cooperatives – were passionate advocates for local, ethical and eco-friendly products, and I knew my co-founder, Halimah, would have cherished associating with them. They viewed the high-street chains as antithetical to their ethos. While David's warning did nothing to dampen my resolve to approach the large chains, it did impress upon me the necessity of treading carefully and being attuned to the sensibilities and values of different segments within the market.

Armed with this knowledge, I continued my concerted efforts to build a solid foundation for Gift. Following my engagement with David, I found myself besieged by a deluge of administrative work, including new product line forms detailing dimensions, weights, price points and profit margins, as well as contracts awaiting my signature.

As March 2013 dawned, Gift received its first distributor order, a modest but momentous milestone. Sales gradually began to climb as more independent retailers brought my products onboard, spurred by Gift's advertisement in The Health Store's catalogue and presence at the Natural Products Europe show. I allowed myself a six-month runway to amass a robust network of retailers and at least one distributor before venturing to approach retail chains.

At the Natural Products Europe show, I found success in securing numerous small independent retailers as potential clients. I even received business cards from buyers representing large retailers, which initially filled me with a hint of hope. Yet, my attempts to follow up post-event were met with a harsh reality. Contrary to my researched methods on courting big retailers and my naive belief that they would be approachable and receptive, I was given a figurative cold shoulder. Their buyers' personal handing over of their business cards had led me to believe that I wasn't stepping into the territory of unsolicited contact. As it so happened, my optimism couldn't have been more misplaced.

At the event, one buyer had expressed interest in receiving a sample pack of my products, which would prompt a follow-up conversation. In response, I carefully put together a sample box wrapped in layers of exquisite turquoise tissue paper and a meticulously folded cover letter, hoping to create a sense of receiving a personalised gift.

A few days post sending the package, I reached out to the buyer. I was connected to a woman whose tone suggested that my call was somewhat bothersome. Nevertheless, I politely informed her that I was following up on my previous engagement with the company's buyer at the Natural Products Show and enquired if she had received my sample box. She curtly asked me to get to the point.

Despite feeling like ending the call right there, I reintroduced myself, described my products and reminded her of the sample package I had dispatched. She responded with an indifference that stung, stating that she received countless samples daily and had likely discarded mine into a bin. She further informed me that her company's stores were well stocked with all the natural sanitary products they needed, suggesting that I could send another sample pack in the autumn when they would be reviewing new ranges. The conversation left me feeling akin to Roald Dahl's Matilda, being reprimanded by the stern Miss Trunchbull. This experience served as a sobering reminder that breaking into the retail big leagues requires not just passion, but also persistence, savvy and a thick skin.

By July, three months after my first exhibition stand, I was back in the Olympia events venue in Kensington, London for the Allergy & Free From Show 2013. This is a consumer show, and I was eager to interact directly with potential customers. My stand was a modest homemade display featuring a single pop-up banner and a table, contrasting starkly with the elaborate professionally branded stands of more experienced exhibitors. However, my quaint two-by-one-metre stand saw such a high footfall over the three-day show that I barely had a moment to breathe. It was a heady blend of exhaustion and exhilaration.

I was overwhelmed by the unexpectedly high response from women enquiring about my products. As I introduced them, these women started to question the inspiration behind Gift Wellness and how it came into being. As I narrated my journey, my audience grew; passing women halted to listen, leading to a crowd gathering.

In a serendipitous twist, during one of my impromptu talks about Gift's journey, a business card was handed to me through the throngs of listeners while a voice asked for a follow-up call post-event. It was only after my speech concluded that I noticed who had handed me the card: none other than the head of category for beauty buyer at a well-known multinational health-food chain. My exhilaration overpowered the physical exhaustion and sore throat from hours of speaking. I realised this watershed moment was a testament to the power of genuine connection and shared values.

Post day one of the show, as I walked down Kensington High Street, I chanced upon a salon offering a Thai foot spa massage and pedicure for £30. Without a second thought, I entered, finding myself sinking into a large leather massage chair with an attached foot spa tub. The next hour was absolute bliss; each long, deep breath I took was filled with satisfaction. The Thai masseuse who attended to me was incredibly skilled, kneading my feet in a way that felt like a reward for the day's exertions.

On the second day, I opted to wear platform shoes, reasoning that the extra height compared to my usual five-foot-three stance in flat shoes would project my voice further across the crowd. Additionally, platforms would spare my toes the strain of me being tipped up on them all day. I sold virtually all the products I'd packed into my Toyota Corolla, amounting to ten cases of each product line, a total of 720 units. The sales comfortably covered the cost of the show and all related expenses. The last twenty or thirty packs, I gave away to passers-by hunting for freebies towards the end of the show and neighbouring stand holders, who typically reciprocated with one of their products.

The Allergy & Free From Show was an unmitigated success, and as I walked away with empty boxes and a heart full of hope, I couldn't help but feel that Gift Wellness had turned a critical corner. The road ahead was undoubtedly lined with challenges, but with each stride, I was coming closer to fulfilling Halimah's dream of making a difference.

Navigating discrimination

Following the exhibition, I afforded myself a couple of recuperative days before making contact with the buyer from the well-known health-food chain who had given me her business card. Upon reaching out, I was asked by the buyer's personal assistant to submit an email introducing my company, brand and product range.

Promptly obliging, I was soon contacted by a junior member of the buyer's team. She expressed enthusiasm and optimism, informing me that the retailer had yet to introduce menstrual products and the company was considering expanding its inventory in this direction. If approved, my products would pioneer the company's feminine hygiene category. She invited me to present a box of samples in person for final approval. Her enthusiasm was infectious and exciting, but as it turned out, it was too good to last.

The bubble of excitement burst all too soon. Upon my arrival for the meeting with the buyer, the woman's demeanour faltered noticeably. I could see that she hadn't expected to meet an Asian woman wearing a headscarf. Born and bred in the West Midlands, I have a distinct English accent, but my name tends to mislead people over the phone, often being misheard as Selene, Elaine or even Lorraine. Typically, this leads to light-hearted clarifications or slightly awkward remarks about my 'sounding English'. This time, however, her reaction was markedly different, unapologetically betraying her disappointment that I wasn't Caucasian.

The meeting swiftly descended into a farce, her initial anticipation devolving into blatant indifference and disregard for my products. Her aloofness was palpable, reflected in her lack of eye contact and stony countenance. My attempts to highlight the unique features of my tourmaline-infused products and the philanthropic angle of my buy-one-gift-one policy were met with curt dismissals. Abruptly concluding the meeting, she informed me that my brand was too new, lacking the established reputation of some competitors under the company's consideration, and suggested I reapply when it gained prominence.

Leaving the meeting, I was a whirlpool of frustration and sorrow. Needing to confide in someone who could soothe my frayed nerves before I took any rash steps, I reached out to Ash, but he was unavailable. Unable to drive while in this emotional state, I called my older brother, Sohail, who has always been a guiding figure in my life, especially since our father's passing.

As I relayed the events to Sohail, I was so overwhelmed I could barely form coherent sentences. I was heartbroken that my race and appearance had seemingly influenced the decidedly negative experience. Patiently listening to my account, Sohail advised against any immediate reactions, asking that I refrain from responding while in my current emotional state. He suggested that I take the night to sleep on it and email the buyer who had first made contact the following morning.

That night was far from restful. The next morning, fuelled by a mixture of anxiety and determination, I drafted an email to the buyer outlining the distressing events of the previous day's meeting. To my astonishment, her response was almost instantaneous. She expressed sincere apologies for any perceived racial discrimination I might have experienced and gave me her word that the matter would be investigated. In addition, she extended a personal invitation for a meeting.

Cautious, but hopeful, I made my way back to the retailer's Nuneaton headquarters. The buyer was genuinely welcoming, an attitude that drastically contrasted with the earlier reception. She seemed truly interested in my products as I presented them nestled in a craft cardboard box, lined with bright teal paper that matched the tissue surrounding the pads. She mentioned having noticed the flock of women at my Allergy & Free From Show booth, a refreshing acknowledgement after the dismissive treatment from her subordinate.

During our meeting, the buyer showed genuine enthusiasm for Gift's mission, appreciated the design of my packages and asked all the right questions. The proposal she offered was to list Gift pads subject to certain terms and conditions, which I agreed to provisionally, provided they were favourable. We explored pricing details, with her specifying a 65% profit margin – considerably above the 50% I had accounted for. However, she informed me that this was standard for high-street chains and retailers. Although the company didn't cover delivery costs, I could incorporate these by implementing a minimum order quantity.

Other requirements were placing an ad in the company's in-store magazine for customer introduction to Gift pads, and mandatory participation in shop promotions, which occur quarterly and whose costs I would partially bear after each campaign. Payment terms, she stated, were non-negotiable at ninety days, given the risk the company was undertaking with a new brand.

Despite the stringent conditions, I knew that breaking into the high street was critical for elevating brand visibility. I accepted, especially as the buyer mentioned she was considering another European brand, and I didn't want to miss this opportunity.

Upon reaching my car, I immediately called Sohail to share the thrilling news. As I relayed my journey, tears welled up, streaming down my cheeks. My father, an immigrant who'd moved to Britain in the early sixties, had faced an incessant tide of racism throughout his life. He had always underscored to us, his children, the necessity of exerting twice the effort of our white peers to gain any recognition. These words, ingrained in us, prepared us for future challenges. In my twenties, armed with this wisdom, I stood up against my first employer when I encountered discrimination at work.

When my children Halimah and Faizaan were just starting school and nursery respectively, I landed a role at a non-departmental government body. This body aimed to regenerate deprived areas of Derby using a government grant. My background in community arts paved the way for my position as a project officer within the quality-of-life team, working towards funding and executing arts and leisure activities in the inner city, a melting pot of diverse ethnicities.

The initial period was fruitful, and my promotion to manage a team of five officers followed the departure of my former boss. However, this positive trajectory was disrupted with a change in senior leadership. The CEO who had hired me retired, and my first encounter with the new CEO was far from welcoming as he critically evaluated my traditional Pakistani attire, the shalwar kameez and scarf. His prejudiced perception of me signalled the start of a difficult period.

Due to his bias, I found myself sidelined from management meetings, which effectively stripped me of crucial information I needed for my role. Within weeks, these unfair conditions led to allegations of incompetence and a subsequent warning. The job I had once thoroughly enjoyed was now a source of overwhelming anxiety, evident when I dropped a cup of tea due to my shaking hands. It was clear I had to respond.

Advised by a union representative, I sought medical leave and utilised this time to build a case against the company. Concurrently, I secured an interview with the National Society for the Prevention of Cruelty to Children (NSPCC) for a fundraising manager position for Derbyshire. I underwent the interview and soon received an offer from the NSPCC.

After resigning from my role, I took the company to court for racial discrimination, supported by a dedicated young barrister from my union. This David vs Goliath battle against the company's legal team resulted in a victory for me, confirming the case of racial discrimination.

This pivotal experience underscored the importance of standing up for myself and others. The sweet taste of victory was tinged with the bitterness of the ordeal, but it emphasised the power of resilience. It was a hard-learned lesson that discrimination has no place in our society, a belief that has shaped my career ever since.

Fast forward from my early career back to July 2013, six months into my business venture, and I received my inaugural order from a major high-street chain. Despite my excitement, the harsh reality was that after accounting for profit margins, magazine adverts, retrospective campaign payments and delivery charges, I was left with little profit. This made it challenging to restock, let alone invest in marketing or expanding my product line.

Despite these hardships, the growing number of independent stores and distributors from countries like the Czech Republic, Latvia, Lithuania, Spain, Germany, Poland and the Republic of Ireland listing Gift products offered a silver lining. Thanks to them, I could cover my business costs and even draw a modest salary.

Endometriosis sufferers and Gift pads

My entrepreneurial journey has always centred around creating a product that could make a positive difference, so when I started seeing chatter on Twitter about how my Gift pads were helping women with endometriosis, I knew I was moving in the right direction. Before these conversations, I had only heard about the condition in passing, without fully grasping its gravity.

For those unfamiliar, endometriosis is a chronic disorder where tissue similar to the womb's lining or endometrium grows outside the uterus, for example on the ovaries or fallopian tubes. Symptoms can vary, but typical signs include lower abdomen or back discomfort, debilitating menstrual cramps, and pain during or after intercourse. Although painkillers and hormone-based medications are often used for symptom management, surgical intervention may also be necessary.

The exact cause of endometriosis is still unknown, with genetics and immune system dysfunction potentially playing a part. Alarmingly, as many as one in ten women in the UK suffer from this condition, and this statistic only considers those formally diagnosed.[19] Ignorant about this disorder previously, I felt compelled to spread awareness and cautiously optimistic about the potential of my product to aid those affected.

A few months down the line, I was excited to run another Gift Wellness stand at the Allergy & Free From Show in London. Here, I noticed the increasing interest in my tourmaline pads. Yet, it wasn't until Kathleen King, a medical scientist and the chair of the Endometriosis Association of Ireland (EAI), reached out to me that I realised the true potential of my product. Kathleen, an endometriosis sufferer herself, was curious about the positive feedback from the endo community regarding my pads.

When Kathleen enquired if the tourmaline pads could help women with endometriosis, I replied, 'I don't know, perhaps some of your members could test them and let me know.' This resulted in twenty to thirty EAI members testing the pads for three months. The feedback was astounding, as every single participant experienced reduced endometriosis-related symptoms while using the pads. This success led to an invitation for me to speak at EAI's annual conference in Dublin, offering me an opportunity to connect with many women who were praising Gift pads and share my story.

Kathleen's endorsement of Gift Wellness sanitary pads marked a crucial moment for my business:

> 'Gift Wellness sanitary pads are the best choice
> for women who suffer from endometriosis,
> as the painful symptoms of the condition
> are often triggered by the harmful chemicals
> contained in ordinary pads. We are therefore
> extremely pleased to endorse the Gift pads
> range and looking forward to working
> with Gift Wellness to raise awareness
> of endometriosis.'

My niece and endometriosis

My niece, Aamenah, an eloquent schoolteacher and endometriosis sufferer, frequently praises the virtues of the Gift pads. Only a few years older than Halimah, Aamenah is part of a close-knit collective of cousins that also includes her siblings, Yusuf and Imaan, and my son, Faizaan. This group has been virtually inseparable since childhood, when they enjoyed frequent sleepovers, developed their own unique language and shared an array of inside jokes.

Aamenah's journey through the labyrinth of endometriosis was fraught with discomfort. It was multifaceted and complex until she found ways to trace and address the roots of her ailment. Upon hearing of Gift's growing endometriosis following, she greeted the news enthusiastically, providing a testament to how the Gift pads transformed her experience with the condition. Her tenacious exploration of unconventional treatments, and the powerful narrative of conquering her ailment that ensued, deeply moved me and inspired an interview to capture her story.

During our conversation, Aamenah unflinchingly dissected her experience. She linked her struggle with self-worth and vulnerability as a woman to her condition. She felt that had she been male, she would have been shielded from endometriosis, which fuelled a resentment towards her femininity. Aamenah believes that the uterus, the hub of femininity housing the second energy chakra, is the seat of sensuality, creativity, pleasure and joy. She theorised that her rejection of these aspects of femininity led to the uterine lining implanting itself elsewhere in the body, triggering severe pain and blocking joy and sensuality, thereby forming a self-perpetuating cycle of survival.

Aamenah's exploration of holistic health led her to adopt an anti-inflammatory, low-oestrogen organic diet. This lifestyle shift, coupled with supportive supplements and Gift anion pads, trimmed her difficult days down to just three a month. These changes, both dietary and emotional, allowed her to manage her symptoms better.

Aamenah, who has successfully found treatments for her own endometriosis symptoms, is now an endometriosis consultant and extends her expertise to help other women using her methods. During the interview, she recounted the story of a client named Tara (a pseudonym). Tara's victim mindset, rooted in the belief that her femininity attracted harm from males, was something Aamenah could relate to and had overcome herself. This belief led Tara to dismiss her feminine strength and conditioned her to suffer in silence, tying in with research that suggests a link between endometriosis and a history of silent endurance of pain due to childhood abuse or constantly prioritising others' needs above personal wellbeing.[20, 21]

Tara's struggle to conceive and her journey through in-vitro fertilisation battered her feminine identity, inciting feelings of inadequacy and guilt for not being able to give her husband a child. Her tendency to suppress her pain, maintain a façade of normality and strive to fulfil her husband's perceived expectations only intensified her condition. Tara's endometriosis symptoms surfaced after her wedding as she strived to fit into her husband's archetype of an ideal woman. Her decade-long struggle to be someone else, coupled with her effort to be the perfect daughter, came from a mistaken belief that other people's happiness was her responsibility.

However, after separating from her husband and returning to her parental home, Tara noticed a significant decrease in her endometriosis pain and symptoms, including a 50% reduction in her bleeding. She attributes this to the healing power of the gentle masculinity from her four brothers and father, a shift that allowed her to stop performing and reassured her of her inherent worth.

Tara's statement reflects this change:

> 'My brothers reminded me that I could have relationships with men where I didn't feel vulnerable. I was their sister; a sister who they could laugh, joke and be silly with. I could be myself. I no longer needed to perform.

> 'After my nervous system relaxed, I finally got into a clearer head space where I began to question why I had even felt the need to perform. I had been given a diagnosis of severe endometriosis. Why hadn't I respected that my body needed time, love and energy? Why was trying to be someone's version of perfect more important than my health? Was it even their version of perfection or was it my perception of what I thought they wanted from me?

> 'So many questions started me thinking about the "victim" mentality that I'd had. Somewhere

in my past, I had decided that the current version of me wasn't good enough. I was an inadequate female. I strived to be the best at every traditionally female role, simultaneously resenting the fact that males dictated what an ideal female was. As I allowed the waves of injustice to wash over me once again, my thoughts automatically went to, "I hate being a woman… men have the better deal… they do this to us."

'I realised in that moment that this thought alone was causing a physical response in me. My heart was beating fast, my shoulders and jaw tensed, I felt almost breathless. This thought pattern was something that occurred multiple times in a day when I felt stressed by daily chores and motherhood duties.

'It was the moment the penny dropped. This was a choice. My thoughts were a choice. Yes, there might be injustices in this world and in my life, but it was my willingness to participate in societal expectations.

'With Aamenah's guidance, I decided to break my thought pattern that led to the same bodily response. I was no longer going to "feel" the injustice. It is and probably always will be there to some degree.

'It was easier said than done. Training my brain to think in a totally different way took practice, meditation and therapy. Creating new neural pathways where gratitude took the spotlight over victimhood. Practising this daily helped immensely. I found light in the smallest situations.

'At first, it seemed silly… "I am grateful for the dimple on my child's cheek," or, "I'm grateful that the sky is blue today." Why hadn't I marvelled at my child's beautiful dimple before? It is adorable and inherited from me. Why hadn't it been a source of wonder and light for me previously? It was right there in front of me every day. I had been so busy focusing on the injustices that I stopped noticing the blessings around me.

'I realised that these small acknowledgments of gratitude were changing my entire perspective on life. Everything felt better. I no longer looked for the injustice in every situation presented to me by my husband. I was grateful for myself too, no longer beating myself up for not being enough. I no longer pushed myself to the point of pain or discomfort. I honoured and appreciated my body. The more I practised this mindset, the closer I got to my goal: an endo-free life.'

Aamenah added:

'There is an element of mind over matter if one delves deep enough. Our thoughts create a physical response in our body. The events in our lives aren't always ideal, but it's our response that determines the outcome. Tara chose gratitude and love over victimhood and anger.'

Through a journey of self-reflection, guided by Aamenah, Tara recognised her thought patterns and created new neural pathways where gratitude took the spotlight over victimhood. She began to appreciate her unique feminine strength, slowly but surely reclaiming her personal power and seeing her condition from a different perspective. Tara saw her pain as an indicator, a call for self-care rather than a punishment or a sign of weakness.

Her newfound understanding allowed her to discard her masks and misconceptions about femininity, instead nurturing a genuine sense of self-worth. Tara started making positive lifestyle changes, focusing on self-care and honouring her body's needs. With therapy and following Aamenah's advice on diet and the use of Gift anion pads, she noted an additional decrease in her endometriosis symptoms.

Tara's story, and countless others like hers, highlights the intricate relationship between our mindsets, beliefs about ourselves and our health. There seems to be a profound connection between endometriosis and one's perception of femininity, suggesting that the condition isn't merely physical, but a culmination of psychological and emotional factors too.

In the same vein as Aamenah and Tara, there are countless women who face the intertwining hardships of endometriosis and complex self-perceptions about femininity. Their narratives indicate that endometriosis is not just a physical condition, but rather a confluence of psychological and emotional elements. This understanding corresponds with research published in the *Journal of Psychosomatic Obstetrics & Gynecology*, which indicates a strong association between chronic endometriosis-related pelvic pain and increased levels of depression, anxiety and perceived stress.[22]

Holistic approaches to managing endometriosis, encompassing diet, lifestyle, emotional wellbeing and the acceptance of femininity, appear to be a significant step towards potentially overcoming this challenging condition. Aamenah's experience, involving an anti-inflammatory, low-oestrogen organic diet and lifestyle adjustments, aligns with findings published in the *Journal of Alternative and Complementary Medicine*.[23] This research proposes that lifestyle modifications, including dietary changes and stress management, may aid in managing endometriosis symptoms.

Furthermore, Aamenah's emphasis on happiness as a key ingredient in her wellbeing echoes sentiments expressed in the field of positive psychology. For instance, the *Journal of Happiness Studies* published a research piece demonstrating a positive correlation between happiness and improved health outcomes, including longevity.[24] This research further corroborates Aamenah's conviction in the powerful role of joy and fulfilment in managing her endometriosis and enhancing her quality of life.

Tara's narrative, notably her struggle with societal and familial expectations, echoes a study in *Social Science & Medicine*.[25] This study delves into norms and expectations' impact on women's health and wellbeing, theorising that societal pressure could lead to psychosocial stress, potentially affecting overall health and possibly exacerbating conditions like endometriosis.

Post-separation from her husband, Tara witnessed a significant decline in her endometriosis pain and symptoms. However, her journey wasn't devoid of obstacles. Her experience resonates with a study published in *Fertility and Sterility*, which suggests that stress might enhance the inflammatory response, thereby worsening endometriosis symptoms.[26] This correlation underscores stress management as a crucial aspect of endometriosis treatment.

Finally, Aamenah's inclusion of Gift anion pads in her holistic health regimen brings to mind a study in

BMC Complementary and Alternative Medicine.[27] This study spotlights the potential benefits of various complementary and alternative medicine approaches in managing endometriosis symptoms. The implication is that Gift anion pads may play a valuable role in an integrative treatment plan for endometriosis.

This research all points to the importance of a comprehensive and holistic approach to managing endometriosis – one that encompasses diet, lifestyle, emotional wellbeing and the reclamation of femininity.

In closing, I extend my profound gratitude to Aamenah and Tara for their courage in sharing their deeply personal narratives, and to the myriad of women who have entrusted me with their experiences. Their resilience and fortitude propel my ongoing mission to create products that enhance women's health and wellbeing. The inspiration I draw from these stories is unending, fuelling my commitment to contribute positively to women's health.

I wish to end this chapter with a reminder: each one of us has the capacity to rewrite our story as a woman and establish a healthier narrative. This transformative journey requires bravery, resilience and an abundance of self-love. Please remember, your femininity is not your weakness – it's your strength.

FOUR

Gift Wellness Foundation

'Let yourself be silently drawn by the strange pull
of what you really love.'
— Rumi[28]

In this chapter, I take you on a heartfelt journey that marks a pivotal period of my life – the establishment and evolution of the Gift Wellness Foundation. This is no ordinary charity; it's a mission fuelled by dedication to tackle period poverty and a vision to improve the lives of women touched by this crisis.

From the foundation's humble beginnings at the launch of the Period Poverty Forum in Derby to setting up the network of period poverty pickup points, I share with you an insider's look into the strategies I carved and challenges I grappled with, as I ventured to fight period poverty here in the UK. The journey has been fraught with obstacles, including political indifference, but these hurdles have not deterred the foundation from reaching out to those in need: homeless women, refugees, schoolgirls, women on low incomes, those dependent on food banks, as well as women's centres and projects.

As I weave this narrative, I take a moment to reflect on the unforgiving Covid lockdown and its manifold effects on the foundation's work, from the sudden surge in demand from food banks to the lamentable loss of retailers. However, the essence of this chapter, and indeed my journey, is leveraging the power of business to create meaningful change and the dogged determination that drives me forward, come what may.

Slow periods in the business could not deter me from donating pads to women in crisis. I met requests from local schools, homeless charities or women's organisations with open arms – this, after all, is the very essence of Gift Wellness. When whispers of a charity sending aid to regions with displaced or impoverished women reached my ears, my fingers were swift to dial its number, urging the organisation to send vans to collect pallets of stock.

The thought of losing something by giving has never shadowed my heart. In Islam, Sadaqah signifies a voluntary act of charity, a pure offering to please God, with no expectation of reciprocation. Yet, when we give, God's generosity knows no bounds. From childhood, this principle has been woven into my being, and my faith affirms that charity mends the cracks caused by sorrow and grief. It brings me nearer to God's embrace, transforming sadness into a luminous, potent energy.

The force of this energy cradles me in a constant sense of contentment, fulfilment and, above all, gratitude. This richness is the currency of love. How can despair clutch my heart when my hands are extended to those whose burdens are heavier than mine? Halimah's spirit always dances beside me, but through charity, her presence becomes tangible. It is a truth reiterated a thousandfold: the more I immerse myself in aiding others, the more life's tapestry enrichens and happiness blossoms in my soul. It's not that I don't feel grief, of course I do, but my grief does not pull me down, it pulls me up.

Launching the Gift Wellness Foundation

Over the course of several years, I found myself seamlessly navigating the balance between managing my social enterprise and investing time in my charity work, an endeavour deeply rooted in the founding ethos of Gift Wellness. Like a pendulum in perpetual motion, I swung between the realms of business and philanthropy. The rhythmic cadence of this movement mirrored the harmony that I was striving to achieve.

When I attended to the affairs of the business, it was with the awareness that its success was instrumental in empowering the charity. Conversely, my time at the Halimah campus brimming with the effervescence of young dreams or supplying products to women in crisis fortified my resolve to continually expand the reach of Gift Wellness. This cyclical dance became the lifeblood of a purpose-driven existence.

However, 2018 brought a notable shift. With the emergence of the #metoo movement and the release of Plan International's eye-opening report on period poverty in schools,[29] Gift Wellness's charitable efforts began to command widespread attention. As the media spotlight grew, an influx of friends and customers came forward, eager to learn how they could contribute to my mission to combat period poverty.

Seizing the opportunity to amplify my brand's impact, I assembled a stellar team of impassioned women. This included my sister Naurin, a fervent community activist, teacher and foster parent, and my daughter-in-law Aneesa, a young mother and international marketing and sales professional with a strong advocacy for women's human rights. Soon after, one of my dearest friends, Joanna West, a local councillor and passionate community activist who had worked closely with me over the years and had been like an aunty to Halimah, joined as a trustee. Together, we envisioned the establishment of a standalone charity that would operate in tandem with Gift Wellness, driving fundraising efforts and bolstering public engagement in our fight against period poverty.

After seeking financial advice, we acted on our shared vision and launched the Gift Wellness Foundation, a registered charity laser-focused on eradicating period poverty. We broadened our scope to reach women in need, both locally and internationally, setting up a website and donation platform dedicated to distributing non-toxic menstrual products to those lacking access or financial means. Our efforts within the UK primarily targeted homeless women, women's shelters, youth hostels, food banks and students. On an international scale, we prioritised the needs of women displaced by war or famine.

With our charity status secured, we were equipped with newfound opportunities to galvanise volunteers, secure funding and scale the work I had previously been undertaking single-handedly. We remained steadfast in our commitment, recognising the monumental potential for making a significant impact. As we built the foundation and fine-tuned our strategy, we encountered hurdles, not least a paucity of political support and the trials of meeting the heightened demands during the Covid lockdown. Nonetheless, our deep-rooted belief in the transformative power of charity and our unwavering resolve to improve the lives of those in need spurred us on to surmount these obstacles.

March 2019 marked a milestone in our journey with the official launch of the Gift Wellness Foundation at the inaugural Period Poverty Forum held in Derby. This event convened a diverse group of local stakeholders, spanning women's charity workers, social workers, health practitioners, teachers, students and parents. United by a common goal, we set about crafting a comprehensive blueprint to tackle period poverty in Derby, fostering a spirit of collaboration to pilot a novel initiative.

As a result of our joint endeavours, we pioneered the introduction of period poverty pickup points across the city, all hosted by dedicated charities and vibrant community projects. Equipped with the necessary menstrual products by Gift Wellness, these organisations would serve as key distributors and signal us when their supplies required replenishing.

We also pioneered a product distribution initiative that served every school in the city. This programme remained in operation until 2021 when the government took up the mantle of providing free menstrual products to schools. It is vital to underscore, however, that for over two years preceding the government's intervention, we had been proactively combating period poverty in Derby, assuring that all organisations and schools had a consistent supply of products. Consequently, we managed to shrink the footprint of period poverty in the city considerably, with only a handful of individuals falling through the protective safety net we had cast.

The dark side of the moon

As I embarked on this journey, my initial naivety was palpable. Like most, I was blind to the harrowing plight of women who had been unjustly cast into destitution. As I delved deeper, the underpinnings of their predicament began to unravel.

Nonetheless, some questions remain stubbornly unresolved, their haunting echoes growing increasingly loud, particularly those regarding men's treatment of women. The thought of men – soldiers and so-called security forces entrusted with the protection of women – coercing them into sex in exchange for food in refugee camps leaves me deeply perturbed. How can these men easily and normatively abuse the vulnerable women in their care or, worse still, use violence and rape as a weapon of war? Who holds these perpetrators accountable?

The deeper I dug into this rotten core, the more sinister the questions became, scrutinising the very essence of these men whose actions seemed to be tacitly sanctioned by other men in power. Blame is often squarely laid on dictators, but I argue that those men orchestrating regime changes from the safety of parliaments or congresses, oblivious to the destruction of millions of innocent lives, bear an equal share of the responsibility. Alongside them should stand the corrupt leaders, who sacrifice their people's freedom for personal gains. I can't help but question, 'Don't they also have mothers, wives, sisters and daughters? How could they overlook such atrocities?'

This feeds into the concept of hegemonic masculinity, where men in power assert values that enforce gender inequality, establishing a hierarchy of masculinities and differential power access.[30, 31] This idea underpins my questioning of why men in power use violence and rape as instruments of war, and how these actions are sanctioned by other powerful men.

The questions reach an even more fundamental level. Why have all major atrocities throughout history, such as genocides, been commanded by men, not women? Why do countries led by women, like Denmark and New Zealand, have the lowest crime rates and the highest quality of life? Why is men's football marred by racist chants and violence, whereas women's football matches emanate joy and family-friendly sportsmanship? On a personal note, what sets men like my husband, son and brothers, who respect and support women, apart from those who choose violence and oppression?

Research suggests that men who indulge in violent behaviour suppress their 'divine feminine' side.[32] As Carolyn M Matthews MD explains in her article for the *Proceedings of the Baylor University Medical Center*, traditional Chinese medicine recognises yin (feminine) and yang (masculine) aspects in everything, each containing elements of the other. Intriguingly, our mitochondria – our cellular energy factories – hold exclusively maternal DNA. Hence, even the most masculine individuals bear a touch of the feminine within their cells, a nurturing aspect drawn from their mothers. Regrettably, qualities such as kindness and gentleness are often construed as weaknesses, further reinforcing the concept of hegemonic masculinity.

In my early managerial years, I was frequently counselled to conceal my emotions, suppress my softer side. However, our maternal instincts, ingrained in women, aid in raising children with love and wisdom, making a mother's lap the child's first vital school. Male leaders who embrace their feminine instincts will inevitably win their people's hearts, embodying true leadership. They are, after all, leading humans, not machinery or livestock. Meanwhile, women continue to suffer the fallout from the heartless games of male leaders who fail to recognise their divine femininity.

In our meetings at the Gift Wellness Foundation, the team and I often found ourselves awash in a sea of such questions and debates. Yet, we couldn't afford to be too swept up in this global maelstrom. Our focus had to remain anchored to our humble yet significant cause: identifying vulnerable women and ensuring they could access menstrual products.

Periods don't pause for pandemics

The onset of the Covid-19 pandemic found our charity still learning to walk. As the crisis escalated, menstrual products began to vanish from supermarket shelves amid the scramble to hoard essentials ahead of the lockdown. This sparked a tidal wave of requests from organisations supporting low-income women.

The team and I worked relentlessly to meet the demands from burgeoning food banks, homeless shelters for women, youth hostels, and refugee and asylum seeker projects, among others. Our effort took on the aspect of a well-coordinated heist, as we swiftly delivered products with covered faces and made hasty exits.

However, one month into lockdown, we recognised a gap: women from certain community groups couldn't access products supplied to food banks or local charities due to lockdown rules that allowed only one family member to run essential errands. This duty usually fell to fathers who were unlikely to be tasked with procuring period products. In Derby, we tackled this by identifying well-connected local women who could serve as hubs for hard-to-reach women in their communities. Despite the initiative's success, its limited scope left me yearning to help similar communities nationwide.

Meanwhile, a network of emergency Covid-19 crisis food banks sprouted in every major town and city. Most were run by men, and my attempts to stress the importance of menstrual products were met with frustrating responses. I was at my wit's end when a call from my friend Shemiza, who lives in Luton, brought a turning point.

Shemiza, a striking beauty, is a creative director with a heart of gold and a passion for diversity and women's rights, a published poet, social activist, award-winning radio producer, broadcaster, lecturer and TV programme producer. Juggling these roles while single-handedly raising six children, Shemiza offered to interview me and promote period poverty awareness among food banks. Her efforts sparked a viral reaction among Covid-19 emergency food banks, and we at the Gift Wellness Foundation found ourselves being pursued for supplies.

It was around this time I learned that the UK, one of the world's richest countries, had almost double the number of food banks than McDonald's restaurants.[33] In parallel to this, Gift Wellness began feeling the pandemic's pinch. Pre-lockdown, I had sold my products through high-street health-food retailers, independent shops and distributors. The lockdown, however, caused me to lose around 90% of my retailers in the first five weeks. A swift decision to pivot Gift Wellness to a B2C business led to the launch of a new Shopify website.

To attract my erstwhile customers, I had to boost my online presence. Through the government's Kickstart Scheme, designed to prevent young people from slipping into long-term unemployment, I hired a team of twenty-eight to help build this presence. Tasked with launching a campaign to tackle period poverty, an event we named Red Rebel Day, this group helped raise awareness and funds for our work.

The inaugural two-day event in March 2021 raised over £25,000, enough to send 250,000 menstrual pads to Yemen and fund various UK activities. For the project's management, we were fortunate to have Neelam Sultan, a compassionate leader and events coordinator from Norfolk, who broke through multiple glass ceilings with grace and conviction.

Confronting the realities of Syrian refugee women

Prior to August 2022, my response to the demand for menstrual products was reactive, largely influenced by the indelible image of distributing pads to refugee women conceived eleven years before in an airport lounge. However, the pandemic revealed the necessity for a sustainable, easily replicable solution. My visit to Lebanon provided the answer.

Requests for free menstrual products from needy organisations in Britain were ceaseless, ranging from food banks and women's shelters to individuals experiencing period poverty. In addition, voluntary student or staff teams were eager to collect period products for distribution. The Gift Wellness Foundation acted as a go-between, but what if there was an automated means to link these groups? Sketching a Venn diagram on the back of a receipt from my hotel in Beirut, I came up with the solution: an app connecting volunteer collectors, organisations needing product and users looking for free product locations.

In Lebanon, I witnessed first-hand the severe realities of life in Syrian refugee camps. The Gift Wellness Foundation's partnership with Reach, a Human Appeal division, enabled the team and me to distribute 500 hygiene kits to refugee women. Comprising of sixteen volunteers, mostly young British female professionals, the Reach team impressed me with their dedication and commitment.

Our stay in Lebanon fostered an extraordinary team bond. The women reminded me of my own daughter, Halimah, particularly a pharmacist also named Halimah from Luton. With her infectious positivity, she kept our spirits high amid the heartrending situations we encountered. Osma, an accountant, felt like a long-lost family member, and her admiration for my TEDx talk, 'A mother's gift to humanity – Period justice',[34] underscored the need for successful role models from minority ethnic backgrounds.

Among others, Raeesa, a student nurse and digital marketing entrepreneur, stood out with her eye for style and keenness for charity campaigning. Despite our busy schedule, she was continuously active on social media, amplifying our work. Aamena, a car rental manager, brought joy to everyone and frequently engaged me in meaningful conversations about my journey. The eagerness of these young women to learn inspired me to intensify my mentoring efforts, despite Covid disrupting my leadership retreat plans for Halimah College girls.

Of the few young men in the group, Imad, a final-year teaching student and charity worker, left a profound impression with his soft-spoken kindness. The Reach group leaders, Zainab and Khalil, epitomised dedication and passion, leading our mission tirelessly, even when most of us fell ill with Beirut belly. Zainab, a young woman in the male-dominated Muslim charity sector, particularly inspired me with her commanding leadership.

On the first day of our week-long mission, the Reach team and I assembled 500 family food packs containing essential items like rice, pasta, oil, lentils and tinned tomatoes – enough to sustain a family for roughly a month. The next day, we delivered these packs to refugee families across six camps in Arsal. As we approached Arsal, the sight of numerous refugee camps scattered across the rugged landscape began to stir intense emotions within me. The higher we ascended, the more camps became visible.

Upon reaching the first camp, I stepped off the coach on to the dusty ground, feeling the hot sun prickling my skin. As wearing sunglasses or other accessories felt inappropriate, I shaded my eyes with my cap, squinting against the harsh light to see the first Syrian refugees emerging from their shelters.

We started to unload the hefty food packages, handing them to the queued refugees. However, the sight of children playing amid this desolation caught my attention. Many wore old, ill-fitting adult sandals, while others had nothing but dust on their feet. So many children, for whom this camp was the only world they knew. Most had been born here, in this supposedly temporary shelter that was erected a decade ago. I was told that many of these children might not survive the harsh winters, with temperatures plummeting and snow piling up to three or four feet.

After the food distribution at the first two camps, I couldn't restrain my tears anymore. Overwhelmed, I broke down sobbing on the coach, covering my face with my hands.

At the following three camps, I had the chance to interview women, something I had eagerly anticipated. My aim was to bring an academic curiosity to these interactions, seeking to illuminate the realities these women faced. Through these conversations, I learned about the many struggles they encountered within the refugee camps.

It became evident that, as is the case elsewhere in the world, if the mother is alright, the rest of the family likely is too. The women were the pillars of their shelters, and as I removed my shoes to enter their homes and listened to their stories, the importance of providing menstrual products became even more pronounced. When their basic needs are met, they can avoid retreating into dependency, instead utilising their innate strength to survive and invent creative ways to protect their families.

During these interviews, I was struck by how such seemingly mundane products, ones we in the West take for granted daily, are crucial in granting these women agency regardless of their situation. One woman I interviewed, Sadiyah, shared her decade-long ordeal. A petite, elegant woman in her thirties, with an oval face, olive skin and large eyes, Sadiyah was eager to tell her story, harbouring a faint hope that maybe it would unlock a door leading out of her dreadful circumstances.

Sadiyah, an articulate woman, had once been a teacher with a bright career. She spoke of her home in Aleppo being bombed, her husband being seized by soldiers and presumed dead, and her flight to a camp near the Lebanon border with her two-year-old daughter. When that camp too was attacked, they fled once more, crossing the mountains into Lebanon. Initially, they were given a small tent, about five square metres, presumably by the UN Aid Agency.

Miraculously, her husband had managed to escape and found her amid tens of thousands of refugee tents after months of searching. They were then moved to the camp in Arsal, where they have remained since. Their daughter, now twelve, harbours dreams of becoming a doctor. They also have two sons, a five-year-old and a toddler, both born in the camp, knowing nothing of life outside.

When I asked Sadiyah if the family wished to return to Syria, she replied, 'No. They would certainly kill my husband and do terrible things to me and my children.' She described how her husband, suffering from anxiety and a physical injury, struggled to find work. When they ran out of food, they would share meals with other households, just enough to feed their children. What resonated most with me was the family's dependence on Sadiyah's resourcefulness and her ability to maintain good relations within the camp during extraordinarily difficult times.

When the opportunity arose to ask Sadiyah and other women in the camp about the challenges they faced regarding menstrual health, I enquired how they managed their periods while trekking, primarily on foot, across the border into Lebanon. Their responses were strikingly similar, as they shrugged their shoulders and cast their eyes to the ground.

'What do you think?' they'd reply. 'We had nothing and had to bleed into our clothes until we found water to clean ourselves.'

When questioned about the frequency with which they were provided menstrual products in the camp, they unanimously answered, 'Very rarely.' Enquiring further, I asked what they used in the camp to manage their periods. Their descriptions painted a harrowing picture of a ceaseless struggle to source or fabricate makeshift menstrual products, from scavenging discarded rags amid the rubble to tearing pieces from their clothing or cutting up baby nappies into strips.

Interestingly, nappies were regularly supplied, but not menstrual products.

Listening to how these women had to employ such desperate measures to manage their periods was heart-wrenching. It dawned on me that supplying menstrual products wasn't just a matter of hygiene; it was about affording these women basic dignity and respect.

The stories of Sadiyah and the other women I interviewed bore witness to the indomitable spirit and ingenuity of refugee women. Despite confronting unfathomable adversity, they persevered in keeping their families united and striving for a better future for their children. Hearing their stories was a deeply humbling experience, and it only bolstered my determination to persist in advocating for the rights and necessities of women and girls in crisis situations.

My encounters with the women in the refugee camps reinforced my belief that the wellbeing of a family is closely tied to the agency of its women to express their needs and, by extension, the needs of the family. I have often raised my voice against discrimination and other obstacles impeding my freedom, so that I could live authentically, but standing in that refugee camp, confronted with the daily tribulations these women endured, I felt overwhelmed. It seemed as though I had plunged into the abyss of human suffering.

It must have been glaringly evident to aid workers that denying women and girls access to menstrual products effectively confined them to their tents. When provided with menstrual products, refugee women are liberated from a plethora of physical and psychological anxieties, enabling them to venture outside their tents with their dignity preserved. They can then apply their resourcefulness and forge vital relationships that benefit their families.

Crucially, their mental health, mood and positivity improve – essential elements since families rely on the women and mothers to be well. When mothers are positive and productive, their families can harbour hope and positivity, and this sentiment permeates the broader community.

Why was there still a dearth of this essential lifeline and a lack of investment in empowering female refugees to reconstruct their lives, families and communities? It seems evident that the character of a society is reflected in how it treats its women; when women's dignity is upheld, they possess the power to revolutionise their lives and the world, creating a better environment for all. Although my mission to Lebanon fuelled my passion and answered numerous questions that had plagued me for years, I was left with a sense of helplessness and frustration. As someone who seeks solutions, this time, I didn't have the answer, as the resolution required dismantling longstanding perceptions about women's agency, held by egocentric, domineering men who would rather perish than engage in open discourse about women's reproductive rights.

According to estimates by the World Economic Forum, achieving gender parity will take over a century,[35] though I can't help but wonder if men were responsible for those calculations. In the meantime, I resolve to collaborate with organisations like Human Relief that are willing to challenge conventional thinking and work towards supporting more women displaced by conflict or poverty and connecting them with transformative resources.

Zareen distributing hygiene kits in Lebanon, Aug 2022

Period Angels

By the time I returned from my enlightening sojourn in Lebanon, I'd already drafted a flow diagram of how the period poverty app would work and sent it to a developer. The following day, brimming with anticipation, I held virtual huddles with my sisters and the Gift Wellness Foundation trustees to brainstorm the app's name. After an enthusiastic exchange of ideas, we unanimously agreed on Period Angels.

I sketched a concept for the logo, envisioning the letter P adorned with angel wings and a halo, and entrusted it to my wonderfully talented niece, Imaan Aslam, my go-to creative genius. Perhaps because we share the same blood, I've always found working with her so effortless. Even before I'd finished explaining my thinking around the idea, she'd got it and suddenly, our words and minds were synchronised. This magical chemistry is most apparent with my siblings, where so much goes unsaid during conversations, because we intuitively know what the other is thinking.

After a delightful to and fro with Imaan on colours and nuances, we finalised the logo for the app.

Period Angels app icon

In September, the Period Angels app officially entered the development phase. The Android version was launched at the end of November, swiftly followed by the Apple version in mid-December 2022. The immediate challenge was to populate the app with volunteers and organisations and spread the word to potential users.

As I write this passage, the Gift Wellness Foundation team is vigorously implementing our communication strategy. We are reaching out to our existing allies, volunteers and customers, urging them to populate the app, and my calendar is brimming with speaking engagements and interviews, where I passionately advocate for Period Angels.

Fast forward to the end goal – by the close of 2023, we aspire to have Period Angels soaring in every major city in England. By 2024, we envision anyone in the clutches of period poverty in the UK to find solace through the app, with free products accessible within a 5-mile radius.

Partnerships are the beating heart of an initiative like this. Among a multitude of collaborations, Qualitas – an NHS training and development consultancy – shines particularly bright. Over the years, I've frequently lent my support to their Pathway to Partnership programme, a remarkable, award-winning journey tailored to fortify the leaders steering our indispensable GP practices. During these sessions, I'm often invited to take the podium as a keynote speaker to emphasise the paramount importance of vision. I share my personal narrative, shedding light on its relevance to these committed practitioners who've navigated through one of the most turbulent epochs in the history of healthcare, inspiring them to perceive their own trials as a 'GIFT'.

In a memorable gathering back in December 2022, I proposed a novel concept: transforming GP surgeries into nerve centres for the collection and distribution of period products. The response was as heartening as it was immediate, with many doctors showing enthusiastic interest. Emboldened by this support, in early 2023, I sat down with Qualitas's trailblazers, CEO Steve Burrows and Head of Strategy and Innovation Caroline Hine. Together, we navigated a path towards an ambitious goal: recruiting at least one GP surgery from each town and city across Britain. This fruitful collaboration marked a significant victory, not just for Gift Wellness, but for Qualitas too. Our joint efforts are a testament to the power of unity and shared vision.

In parallel, the Gift Wellness Foundation team's good-will continues to reach far and wide, through donations to food banks and charities in Britain, and crossing borders with aid containers. During emergencies like the Pakistan floods in 2022, we collaborated with local charities to either send products or financially support them to purchase locally.

Of course, buying locally presented a double-edged sword, the advantages being supporting the local economy and minimising our carbon footprint, but the flip-side was a severe compromise on the quality of products and our principles. Yes, we would be able to supply more in quantity, as local items would be cheap, but at what cost to the environment and women's health? Plus, we would be promoting brands whose principles we vehemently disagreed with.

This dilemma begs for long-term solutions. Never-theless, accountability is key. I make sure every Gift Wellness Foundation penny is accounted for with photos, videos and documents as evidence.

This journey, my dear readers, is a tapestry of dreams, resolve and collaborations, woven together to combat period poverty. Onward we march!

FIVE

Charting New Waters

'Out beyond ideas of wrongdoing and rightdoing,
there is a field. I'll meet you there.'
— Rumi[36]

As my journey progressed, it became increasingly clear that to effect meaningful change, one must dare to venture into uncharted territories. This chapter is a tapestry woven from threads of innovation and the ever-evolving strategies of marketing, demonstrating their collective force in driving positive transformation in our world.

We embark by turning our attention to an issue that resonates profoundly with most of us – the environmental crisis. For me, the imperative to address the deluge of plastic suffocating our planet led to a vision: plastic-free bathrooms. Through a window into the development of my cleansing bar range, you will be privy to the meticulous research and development that birthed Gift's sustainable alternatives. In addition, I share my thoughts on the importance of sustainable products for inner-city communities and refugee camps.

In the next section, innovation takes the forefront once again as we explore its potential in championing reproductive rights. The launch of the Period Gift Box was spurred by probing questions and a desire to address the menstrual challenges experienced by schoolgirls. As the chapter progresses, I'll touch upon the cultural and health benefits of washing after using the toilet and make a bold proposition – to utilise VR technology to engender more female-inclusive work environments, while also advocating for the provision of free menstrual products in workplace washrooms.

As we traverse further, the kaleidoscope of marketing comes back into focus. We'll chart its metamorphosis from traditional avenues to the ascent of social media, influencer endorsements and the advent of AI. Moreover, we'll examine the discourse around employing gender-neutral language. We reflect upon its pertinence and clarify the rationale behind its ultimate exclusion from Gift's marketing approach.

In essence, this chapter serves as a testament to the sheer magnitude of what can be accomplished when innovation is harnessed with astute marketing strategies. It is about the alchemy of creativity, diligence and strategic acumen in not only realising your objectives, but also imprinting lasting, positive change upon the tapestry of the world.

The expansion of the Gift Wellness product range was nothing short of meteoric – a leap from a modest three products to an astonishing assortment of around thirty, all within a mere two-year span. This transpired in the wake of my pivotal decision to shift Gift's sales strategy from high-street retailers to a direct online B2C model. Conventional wisdom would dictate trepidation in the face of such a monumental overhaul, having to virtually restart the business anew, but fortified by my unyielding faith and the conviction that events unfurl in harmony with a grander design, I remained undeterred. I embraced the certainty that if the intentions steering my endeavours were anchored in integrity, the tide would turn in my favour.

There was an ethereal quality to the zeitgeist as a multitude of elements converged into a perfect storm, including the redirection of my business trajectory, the imposition of the Covid lockdown and the sudden escalation in demand for addressing period poverty. Serendipitously, in the months preceding the lockdown, Ash and I had been tirelessly breathing new life into the lower level of our home. Our labour of love culminated in an open-plan sanctuary; a haven imbued with warmth from a crackling log burner and a panoramic glass expanse that blurred the lines between indoors and the verdant embrace of our garden. In this tranquil refuge, it felt as though the universe conspired to endow me with the ideal crucible for creativity and innovation to flourish unbridled.

Towards conscious consumption

For quite a while, my thoughts had been percolating around the assortment of products I yearned to introduce, and one notion remained unequivocally lucid – shampoo bars devoid of plastic are imperative. As governments across the globe engage in ceaseless deliberations concerning the array of looming threats, from pandemics to terrorism and where the next regime change is needed, I stand firm in my conviction that it is the scourge of plastics in the environment that casts the darkest shadow over humanity's future. In an alarming report, the environmental custodian, Oceana, divulged that in 2022, our oceans were besieged by plastics to the tune of two garbage trucks per minute – a staggering 33 billion pounds annually.[37]

My dear Halimah's passion for climate change issues was palpable. In pursuit of her calling, she was set to dedicate her second year at university to environmental conservation and poverty alleviation projects in The Gambia. Our faith ingrains in us a sacred duty to be stewards of the Earth; to shield its verdant splendour and the myriad lives it cradles. Even in conflict, the sanctity of nature is paramount – no tree may be felled, no creature harmed. We are bequeathed guardianship and will be held accountable before the Divine for every handful of Earth we destroy.

This tenet renders it profoundly disheartening to witness a palpable disconnect within segments of my own community. Inner-city areas, particularly those inhabited by ethnic minority communities, appear besieged by environmental transgressions, and at the crux is a disconcerting truth – a dearth of investment in environmental education for marginalised communities, a testament to the government's flagrant disregard for empowerment through knowledge.

Eminent climate scholars have drawn a grim correlation between environmental degradation and poverty. The wealthier echelons of society bear the brunt of culpability for ecological misdemeanours, yet it is the impoverished who suffer the consequences. This insidious paradigm has been dubbed by climate activists the 'new colonisation', a sinister stratagem to control the masses and subjugate the vulnerable, perpetuating the chasm between the wealthy and the destitute.

As a passionate advocate for change, I believe it is incumbent upon all of us with the means to do so to dispel the ignorance, empower through education and reclaim the sanctity of our shared home.

In the quaint town of Dudley during the 1970s, my family home was affectionately adjoined to a charming corner shop… yes, we had a corner shop! My father's keen eye for emerging products at the cash and carry meant the shop served as our very own testing ground. I can still picture him unveiling the magical wonders of cling film to my mother as he deftly enveloped a bowl of daal and performed an audacious inversion. As it did in most households, this humble innovation swiftly gained an indispensable status in our kitchen.

My reminiscence drifts back to my tender years, as a five- or six-year-old, being bathed by my doting aunt using a bar of soap. However, a transformative moment was on the horizon as she one day introduced a plastic bottle of body wash, which took pride of place on the bathroom shelf, heralding a new era. As adolescence graced my sisters and me with its bounties and tribulations, the pursuit of perfect hair beckoned an array of shampoos and conditioners and we would eagerly experiment, seeking the product that would provide the silkiest result. As teenage spots appeared, so did many variants of face wash, all packaged in enticing plastic bottles.

Anita Roddick's Body Shop burgeoned as a beacon of ethical enterprise in the mid to late eighties, introducing to us the concept of a business for good, and we wanted to be part of her tribe.[38] Though her ethos encouraged the return of Body Shop plastic containers for recycling, our adherence wavered between doing so and forgetting to, as the allure of a new bottle of Tea Tree Oil facial wash beckoned.

As my cognisance of environmental concerns developed, particularly during the introspective silences of the lockdown, my reflection retraced the steps of these evolutionary shifts in our consumption. My sisters and I, as teenage consumers, had unwittingly capitulated to the narrative woven by corporate giants, as our bathrooms transformed into plastic-laden sanctuaries. We were lambs to the slaughter, enticed by the glamour of television advertisements, ensnared into a pursuit of the latest and greatest. Our dear father, a man of boundless generosity, wished for nothing but to fulfil our hearts' desires. As I reminisced, it became apparent how pivotal it is to critically evaluate our choices, and to empower ourselves and future generations to foster sustainability and conscientious consumption.

When I conceived the idea of the Gift Wellness range, I was confronted with a similar narrative as mainstream menstrual products were swathed in plastic. At the inception of Gift pads, alternatives to plastic were still nascent and unaffordable, which would have hindered accessibility to my products, and I yearned for them to be within reach for everyone. Consequently, the initial designs incorporated plastic in the adhesive layer that would be stuck to underwear and the wrapper for individual pads, though the outer packaging box was paper based. However, my inexperience led me to opt for a glossy finish for the boxes for my first container of stock. Only later did I discover that the shine was achieved using a thin layer of plastic film.

As my consciousness about hidden plastics expanded, and as alternatives became more economical, I was enthralled to witness the Gift pad range's metamorphosis towards an increasingly plastic-free lineage. I harboured a sense of scepticism regarding claims from other brands about their pads being much better for the environment because they were entirely plastic free and compostable. The journey of a pad, no matter how plastic free, was that it would usually be disposed of in the bathroom bin, then transferred to the main mixed bin, and then of course to a landfill site. Let's face it, the final destination of used pads and tampons was never going to be a compost bin; they were destined for landfills.

Conversely, Gift Wellness pads stand apart for their environmental benefits. Our pads are at least six times more absorbent than ordinary ones and are toxin-free, with the addition of tourmaline mineral to regulate the menstrual cycle. This unique composition allows for a more fluid menstrual flow, eliminating the typical stop-and-start effect caused by toxic supermarket pads. Customers report that their periods become on average one-third shorter, reducing pad usage and consequently landfill contributions. By ensuring a shorter, more comfortable cycle and cutting down waste, Gift pads make a genuine difference both for women and the planet.

My driving force is anchored in ensuring that my products are the best thing for women's health and wellbeing. Serendipitously, what has emerged as beneficial for women is also the best thing for the planet. This journey illuminates a profound realisation. When the wellbeing of individuals is placed at the forefront, the ripple effect invariably propagates positive outcomes across all spectra, including the environment.

Paving the way to plastic-free bathrooms

It is staggering how recycling, a routine practice in kitchens, often doesn't extend its reach to bathrooms, where an alarming proportion of plastic is heedlessly disposed of with general waste. A substantial 30,000 tonnes of recyclable bathroom waste is recklessly relegated to landfills annually. Notably, this can be attributed to the fact that over half of the UK population confesses to discarding recyclable items as regular trash.[39] Visualise the monumental impact on reducing plastic waste if we rewire our thought process on this matter.

Embarking on the creation of my soap bars, which I resonated more with calling 'cleansing bars', I was unequivocally resolved that they, like my pads, would transcend the ordinary. Alongside mitigating environmental degradation, my cleansing bars would be a balm for the skin and hair. My sisters, the trusted first line of feedback for any new product, were my confidants in this venture.

My sister Saiqa, having grappled with psoriasis since youth, posed a query, 'Won't soap dry my skin out?'

I replied, asking her what didn't dry out her skin. Her response was an epiphany; she divulged that Epsom salts baths on alternate nights were her sanctuary.

Armed with this insight, I liaised with a soap artisan in Dorset and my most trusted packaging designer, my niece Imaan, to manifest my vision. The composition of my range was an ensemble of coconut oil, pure essential oils and Epsom salts, eschewing detrimental elements found in conventional soaps, like palm oil, parabens and synthetic fragrances. The repertoire encompasses shampoo, conditioner, body wash, face wash, hand wash and intimate wash bars, as well as an amalgamation of these – the all-in-one bar.

The concept of decluttering bathrooms of a plethora of plastic bottles and replacing them with a singular bar is exhilarating. Saiqa's favourite is the intimate wash bar, due to its pH-neutral formula, minimalist ingredients (coconut oil, organic apple cider vinegar and Epsom salts) and evocative scent reminiscent of the previous harvest of apples.

I yearned for these products to catalyse a societal metamorphosis, commencing within my immediate circle. A seismic shift rendering cluttered plastic-laden bathrooms obsolete and unfashionable. Envision a scenario where a guest at a friend's home, after using the bathroom, candidly exclaims, 'Why is your bathroom swarming with plastic? That's so passé!'

What swells my heart with pride regarding the cleansing bar range is not just its environmental merit, but its triumph in efficacy over liquid counterparts. Customers rave about the extended longevity of the shampoo bars, the indulgence reminiscent of a spa experience and the sheer fulfilment derived from minimising plastic wastage. The vision has metamorphosed into tangible change.

Gift shampoo bar

Empowering daughters with the gift of confidence

As I immersed myself in my mission to furnish free products to women in turmoil, a facet of period poverty persistently gnawed at me. My perception of the gravity of this predicament intensified upon my perusal of the 2018 Plan International report accentuating the impact of period poverty in schools.[40] The report was a jarring revelation, indicating that numerous schoolgirls were prevented from reaching their full potential due to period poverty. With 42% of girls in Britain resorting to makeshift sanitary products and 27% stretching the use of products beyond their safe tenure due to financial constraints, the figures were alarming.

Perhaps the most distressing reality was that many girls began menstruating while in school, some at the tender age of eight or nine, in an abyss of unawareness. It was heartbreaking. The anguish and confusion at such an innocent stage could potentially wreak havoc on their confidence, mental wellbeing and academic strides.

This provoked an imperative interrogation of what pre-emptive measures could mitigate this scenario. What solutions could I conjure? I ruminated, 'What tools do parents need to effectively support their daughters through the advent and progression of their menstrual journey?'

My brainchild was the revolutionary Period Gift Box. This exquisitely curated treasure trove teems with premium natural products and enlightening resources. However, it transcends a rudimentary starter kit. The cornucopia encompasses an assortment of delights including Gift pads, intimate wash bar, a beautifully bottled calming aromatherapy perfume and a natural heat pad crafted from rice and organic French lavender. Chocolate, the quintessential indulgence, is a mandatory inclusion! Pivotal to the Gift Box is a suite of cards mimicking text messages on a smartphone, tendering invaluable advice and insights in a light-hearted yet impactful manner to mums, dads, siblings and the young recipients themselves.

I am acutely conscious that period poverty encompasses more than financial impediments, as cultural and emotional barricades that thwart girls from accessing necessary products are equally culpable. This trailblazing solution eradicates the harrowing introduction to menstruation for girls. The transformation was profound, from girls experiencing a state of mortification and powerlessness to empowerment and mastery over their cycles and emotions.

The Period Gift Box burgeoned into a beacon of solace and gratitude, amassing stellar accolades from parents post its launch. Supplementing the Gift Box, I introduced Planet Period on the Gift Wellness website, a reservoir of answers and resources on menstruation for parents, educators and children.

The Period Gift Box transcends a mere commodity; it symbolises a crusade for metamorphosis. Through education and empowerment, I endeavour to eradicate the manifestation of period poverty, unleashing the limitless potential in girls. The Period Gift Box is an offering that amalgamates essential menstrual products, wisdom and the fortitude that equips these young blossoms to triumph in every sphere of their existence.

Cultivating female-friendly workplaces

Post the pleasing strides in supporting schoolgirls, my compass pointed towards the labyrinth of challenges women face in their professional spheres while navigating their natural reproductive bodily functions. Astonishingly, no consultancies offered equalities training that specifically addressed this issue, despite industry experts from McKinsey and Forbes to Harvard discussing the need for gender parity in the workplace.[41]

This epiphany birthed Female Friendly Workplaces (FFW), a specialist consultancy which recognised the void in critical professional development within organisations that aim to create such workplaces. Despite an earnest intent to close the gap, bereft of a concrete starting point, these organisations floundered in attaining their equality objectives. The time was ripe for a groundbreaking solution, one capable of dispelling the enigmatic stigma surrounding women's health in an affable and enjoyable way.

The task at hand was to dismantle the age-old taboos enveloping women's reproductive health – menstruation, pregnancy, menopause and affiliated conditions. FFW's concept was to harness the power of VR, creating an immersive solution that would advance women's equality in the workplace by developing empathy, respect and inclusion. The approach resonated with industry and government objectives to improve gender equality and inclusion in the workplace, with a particular focus on science, technology, engineering and maths industries, and beyond.

FFW's immersive tutelage is unparalleled, specifically tailored to address women's reproductive issues within professional settings, an offering to be found nowhere else in the contemporary market at the time of writing. VR materialised as my instrument of choice, stemming from the realisation that a tectonic shift was imperative to initiate discourses surrounding women's reproductive functions within corporate corridors, a topic conventionally shunned. VR offers a conduit to dispel misconceptions and undertake decisive strides in normalising conversations around the needs of women in workplaces without causing the discomfort or embarrassment of face-to-face interactions.

My VR modality employs Oculus gaming headsets, transporting delegates into virtual workspaces to walk in the shoes of a female colleague as she deals with various situations. One scenario depicts Maria, on the cusp of delivering a pivotal presentation. Confronted with her employer outside the conference room, the participant is presented with three options and asked, 'What should Maria do?' The alternatives posed: come clean and confess, fabricate an excuse, or say nothing and soldier on. By gamifying the exercise, we made the issue accessible and non-confrontational. Six scenarios, crafted with veritable actors and 360-degree cameras, emerged thanks to the film-making mastery of the team at Spark Media in Birmingham.[42] To strike equilibrium, half portrayed men grappling with mental health, invisible disabilities and paternity leave.

FFW's pioneering VR endeavour breaks new ground, necessary to achieve genuine workplace equity. The immersive experience accords an intimate glimpse into the tribulations that women weather, fostering an understanding which transcends theoretical wisdom. My enterprise unveils a unique opportunity to address taboo subjects and create more inclusive workplaces, catering to women's needs to the mutual benefit of them and the organisation as a whole.

FFW's VR innovation nurtures empathy, understanding and inclusivity, laying the groundwork for employees to experience life from the perspective of others, dismantling age-old taboos and cultivating congenial surroundings. It empowers organisations to gain a holistic grasp of the multifarious needs of their staff, metamorphosing their stance on gender equity and inclusiveness, thereby bringing about a fundamental shift in workplace culture.

Since FFW's inception through scribbles on a mind-map amid the Covid lockdown, my unflinching conviction remains that my cutting-edge innovation is an undeniable imperative in the creation of fair and nurturing work environments. By empowering organisations with the acumen to discern and tackle the challenges women encounter, my solution paves the way to a culture of comprehension, veneration and empathy, metamorphosing workplaces for posterity. Monumental leaps towards gender parity and inclusiveness are then conceivable.

In December 2021, the spark of the FFW training consultancy began to blaze as I delivered a demo to the management of a company in London, which was knee-deep in the construction of a bank in Canary Wharf. The exercise resonated deeply with the participants, who offered invaluable feedback based on their experiences, helping my team and me refine our scenarios.

My research revealed the powerful impact of VR in ensuring people would retain information, positioning it as a remarkably effective tool for professional development and awareness of reproductive rights. It's a simple truth: reading or hearing about an experience pales in comparison to living it, even virtually. PwC's 2020 report, 'Seeing is believing', predicts a global gross domestic product increase of US$1.5 trillion by 2030 due to immersive technologies.[43] The study shows that trainees using VR are not only faster to learn, but more emotionally engaged with the content. They are 275% more confident to apply the skills they have learned and four times more focused compared to e-learning alternatives. This is among many reports that underscore how VR, by evoking emotional and cognitive empathy, can foster compassionate actions. FFW's demos reflect this – a single virtual experience can be eye-opening and inspire people to think and act differently.

This is no mere checkbox exercise. FFW aims to be the backbone of an integrated strategy within an organisation's culture. The FFW consultancy supports employers and HR departments in crafting environments that are more receptive and accommodating to women. This, in turn, helps bridge the gender gap and ensure balanced representation.

Although the concept of FFW is solid, the execution was among the most complex endeavours I had ever embarked upon. However, it was worth every ounce of effort, as the outcome has developed into a groundbreaking programme that could be a turning point for any organisation.

Providing period products in
workplace washrooms

With the ball rolling on the FFW initiative, it became clear that the next crucial step was urging employers to offer free menstrual products to female employees. I mean, how can we talk about women flourishing in the workplace if they don't even have access to the essentials during their period?

The hunt for a solution began. I quickly realised that giving out free period products is an easy and inexpensive way for employers to show they care about making the workplace better for women, so my team and I spruced up our Gift Wellness website with a section called 'Workplaces'. There, we offer nifty dispensing machines that dole out pads and tampons at no cost in the workplace bathrooms.

Our dispensers are built to be user-friendly and a breeze to take care of. They're a one-time buy that fits right in, whether the environment is a school or a swanky corporate office. Plus, with a monthly subscription service keeping the dispensers stocked, women and girls can always rely on having the products they need on hand.

I am beaming with pride over this straightforward yet powerful solution. It has the makings to change how women perceive their employers and their workplaces. No more stressing about periods catching them off guard, they are imbued with a newfound confidence, knowing their wellbeing matters to their employer. Together with employers, we're raising the banner for period equality and laying the groundwork for a workplace culture that's more inclusive and caring.

Another splash of inspiration

'To wash or to wipe?' Behold, the age-old question that's haunted the minds of bums since time immemorial. I know some might think it's mere toilet trivia, but hear me out. The way we tend to our behinds post-throne session can make or break our personal hygiene.

Cue in a nifty invention that's still simmering on a back-burner: the wall-mounted intimate wash foam dispenser. Why it's not rocking the shelves yet is thanks to a mix of costs, the intricate dance of installation and some cultural side-eyes. My vision is simple – to nudge folks, especially women, to opt for a gentle wash instead of a hasty wipe when they make a pit stop at the loo.

I get it; the subject is a tad... delicate (wink), particularly in the West. In Asian, Middle Eastern and Mediterranean lands, skipping the wash and only wiping would raise eyebrows and provoke an 'Eek!' For these cultures, washing is such a staple; it's no wonder the toilet paper frenzy during the Covid lockdown didn't hit local Pakistani shops that hard.

Let's get down to the butt of why not washing the undercarriage is a bad strategy for women. One: dry tissue swipes spread the nasty bacteria squad, with chances of them gate-crashing your urinary tract – not a party you want. Two: overzealous wiping? Hello, irritated skin and the not-so-jolly rashes, especially if your toilet paper is like sandpaper with a dash of harsh chemicals.

Here's the bottom line: embrace washing. You'll be a hero to trees too (less paper frenzy) and no more toilet bowls choked in a paper entanglement. Plus, your precious behind that puts in the work daily gets the VIP treatment it deserves. Quick reality check: if poo made an accidental cameo elsewhere on your body, would a tissue dab cut it? I think not.

Now for the 101: grab a jug and park it by the toilet, ready to be filled with some cosy warm water. Then, it's the teamwork of your hands – the right one pouring, while the left one does the clean-up. Pat yourself dry with tissue and, of course, a thorough hand wash afterwards is the closing act.

Though my foam wash is on hold, my battle-cry for wash facilities, especially in schools and workplaces, is loud and clear. It's high time for a cultural shift, like installing sinks in toilet stalls, making it smooth sailing for menstruating gals. This is an all-out diversity and inclusion flag, especially for those of us with a washing ritual. No need to throw our traditions to the wind and wander around feeling like a hot mess.

Next time you're on the porcelain throne, mulling over whether to wash or to wipe, know that a splash of water and soap is like a hygiene high-five to your bottom. Cheers to pristine posteriors everywhere!

Navigating the evolving landscape of marketing

When Gift Wellness sprouted into existence in 2012, I was blissfully unaware that I had set sail on the choppy waters of a marketing world on the brink of an overhaul. My compass was firmly set towards traditional advertising shores – think magazine ads, posters, flyers and newspaper features. These tactics hit the bullseye for customers who were no strangers to high-street retail outlets and indie health stores, but as time galloped forward, I realised I needed to evolve to stay in the game.

The 2020 Covid pandemic was a curveball, not just for me, but for the world. Like a magician pulling rabbits out of a hat, I swiftly transitioned Gift Wellness to an all-online e-commerce star ship. I bid adieu to ink on paper and welcomed digital embraces through blog posts and social media chitchat. Gift Wellness's YouTube channel flourished with heartfelt video testimonials from customers, along with a crown jewel – my TEDx talk called 'A mother's gift to humanity – Period justice'.[44]

Still, the marketing kaleidoscope continued to shift. By the end of 2022, my social media endeavours were great for brand banter, but weren't opening the sales floodgates. A fresh recipe was needed. After a one-to-one early in 2023 with my business guru Daniel Priestley,[45] my lens focused on good old face-to-face marketing – speaking at events to live audiences, being interviewed on podcasts and mingling with influencers.

Emerging from being locked-down, we humans were all wired for connection, yearning for raw and authentic eye-to-eye conversations. There's magic in stories shared with warm smiles, a far cry from the pixelated Zoom life. The pandemic was like a slingshot, pulling us back only to catapult us towards a hunger for live experiences. Storytelling became our elixir, a reminiscent echo of our ancestors around campfires.

Reading a book is like having a heart-to-heart talk, so this book has taken centre stage in my marketing ballet. It's my soul poured into pages aimed at resonating with readers, like we're holding hands through ups and downs. Trust, kinship and understanding are what I seek to cultivate.

Then came another layer of adaptation – the tapestry of cultural diversity. A call for gender-neutral language and imagery tugged at me. While my heart beats for equal rights and diversity, I have to keep my compass aligned with my target audience. It was like walking a tightrope. My resolve? Staying steadfast in championing women's human rights, while offering an open door for anyone in need of Gift products, irrespective of gender.

Enter stage right, ChatGPT, a blazing star in the AI cosmos.[46] ChatGPT is like having a personal genie helping create social media posts, answer customer questions and more, but every silver lining has a cloud. While ChatGPT whizzes through tasks, concerns about job displacement and misuse, such as spinning fake news, hover in the air. Nonetheless, ChatGPT is like my digital sidekick, bolstering my content and customer service. While it may not don the cape for face-to-face marketing, it's a powerful ally in enhancing marketing strategies and customer encounters.

This ever-shifting marketing odyssey has been a roller coaster, but oh, the gems of wisdom I've gathered! Marketing is akin to alchemy, blending product promotion with forging bonds and nurturing communities.

As Gift Wellness sets sail into the horizon, my heart is ablaze with anticipation. We all stand on the cusp of harnessing marketing strategies and tech that can stitch hearts closer together and cultivate enduring bonds. The road might be paved with challenges, but with unflinching passion, dedication and an unwavering commitment to period justice and women's health, I stand undeterred, ready to embrace the future.

In essence, marketing is akin to riding an ever-changing sea, demanding nimbleness and creativity. Through thick and thin, Gift Wellness remains anchored in purpose, with sails set to chart unexplored waters, driven by the winds of passion for natural health and wellness. Here's to navigating the waves together!

SIX

It's Not Just Business, It's Personal

'Your acts of kindness are iridescent wings of divine love, which linger and continue to uplift others long after your sharing.'
— Rumi[47]

A s this book draws to a close, my heart swells with gratitude for the meandering path that led me to this very moment. In this concluding chapter, I distil the essence of the priceless lessons I've gathered along the way and unveil the GIFT method – a potent elixir to ignite the fire within, equipping you to weave a future that's not only socially aware, but also leaves an indelible mark.

Throughout the chapters of this book, you've walked with me through tales of innovation, marketing, mentorship and blooming personal growth. As we step into this final enclave, I share my vision for a future steeped in social consciousness and extend my hand, inviting you to journey alongside me. We've traversed the realms of transcending limitations, sculpting positive ripples and staying anchored in one's core values. Now I want to underscore the necessity of fusing business and personal values as the very fabric of crafting a socially conscious future for yourself, one that inherently rests on uplifting others.

Enter the GIFT method, a tapestry woven with threads of gratitude, illustrate, focus and triple bottom line. Envision it as the first step on an enriching odyssey, a compass guiding entrepreneurs to crystallise their raison d'être, paving the way to triumph and leaving an imprint that resonates through generations. This symphony of the mind and heart ensures that your journey is steeped in authenticity, your sails set with unwavering intent.

With gratitude as your anchor, visualisation as your map, focus as your compass and the triple bottom line as your guiding star, you harness the tempests of sorrow, trauma and strife, morphing them into gales that steer you towards a horizon ablaze with purpose and zeal. Once your venture takes wing, let the GIFT method be the beacon in your business plans and reflections, an enduring tether to your founding aspirations as you wade through the waters of entrepreneurship.

In this metamorphosis towards socially conscious entrepreneurship, it is imperative to weave threads of compassion into the fabric of your business blueprint. A new dawn has arrived, with discerning, socially astute consumers in search of products that echo their values.

At its heart, this book is a celebration of the invincible spirit of positivity, love and the endless chase of grand dreams. May it kindle in you the audacity to embark upon your own monumental adventure, to chase your star and to sculpt a legacy that reverberates through the ages. As a parting gift, I unfurl the secret tapestry behind the title of this book, *The GIFT*, and unveil the treasure it holds so close to my heart.

If you have read this far in the book, having held my hand as I hauled you through the heartbreak and rejoiced with me as I rose to new heights, lifting your spirits with mine in celebration, then I must thank you as I share my final thoughts. I propose that it is time to rethink the traditional approach to achieving entre-preneurial goals and embrace a more purpose-driven, impactful and collaborative one.

Conventional wisdom dictates that the sole focus of business should be maximising profit in the shortest time possible, often at the expense of broader con-siderations. However, my own odyssey was set in motion from that serendipitous moment of clarity at Lahore airport. There, I was consumed by a vivid scene of myself distributing vital products to women in refugee camps, my soul ablaze with the desire to forge positive change through humanitarian ventures.

Inspired by an unwavering commitment to honour the promise I made to Halimah and driven by a fervour that surpassed my lack of business acumen, I embarked on crafting a venture where altruism was not an afterthought, but the very foundation. This orientation served as a compass, ensuring that the facets of my business were in harmony with my core values.

My ambition was to architect something that would emit an aura of positivity and healing akin to the tourmaline in my pads, counterbalancing the forces of negativity and leaving an indelible benevolent imprint on the world. The ethos of a social enterprise, constructed on a bedrock of kindness, resonated deeply within me.

The triple bottom line concept, which I have incorporated as the final step of the GIFT method, is an elegant balance between people, planet and profit championed by Harvard Business School.[48] It argues that a company's pursuit should extend beyond monetary gains and encompass social and environmental stewardship. My curiosity was piqued: why were more businesses not adopting such a holistic approach? The superiority of social enterprises over their conventional counterparts is as clear as day. Recalling conversations with Halimah, contrasting the conventional capitalist mould with that of social enterprises, I further fortified my resolve.

The prevailing wisdom holds businesses hostage to the notion of relentlessly chasing profits, often with blinkered disregard for the repercussions. However, infusing your business model with elements of philanthropy, social impact and cooperative endeavour from the outset not only serves as a linchpin for aligning your deeds with your ideals, but also shepherds your business along a path of moral integrity as it flourishes. As my entrepreneurial saga illustrates, this alternative blueprint for business is not just viable, but profoundly transformative.

Embracing collective morality in a competitive world

In his seminal work, *Morality*, former Chief Rabbi Jonathan Sacks underscores the imperative of veering towards a society that is more synergistic, where the ethical compass is calibrated to the collective 'we' rather than the insular 'I'.[49] He astutely remarks that the contemporary global market, propelled by an unrelenting quest for power and affluence, often falls short on the scales of equity and morality. This imbalance gives rise to societal quandaries including poverty, burgeoning debt in emergent nations and movements that unmask pervasive injustices, such as #metoo.

Sacks advocates for a paradigm shift – from a society steeped in individualism to one that embraces collectivism, fostering trust and collaboration among its constituents. He accentuates the necessity to champion the common good, transitioning from an I-centred worldview to a we-centred tapestry of shared values and objectives. In the context of our contemporary age, unrestrained capitalism has woven a tapestry that is at times grim and tyrannical, where the mighty often exploit the defenceless – a reality laid bare by movements like #metoo and the disparities that plague our legal systems.

Sacks elucidates that while the relentless pursuit of wealth and power can often birth divisions and foster a culture of resource hoarding, there exist treasures that defy this mould. Knowledge, skills, love, friendship and influence are imbued with a moral and spiritual essence that sets them apart. These treasures burgeon not through concealment, but through dissemination. When we disseminate these invaluable treasures, we sow the seeds of unity, advancement and rejuvenation. As they are shared, their worth multiplies and their impact cascades boundlessly.

In a world where the business landscape is often synonymous with competition, morality extols the virtues of collaboration. It invites us to look beyond the narrow confines of personal glorification, and instead cultivate a society that holds collaboration and generosity in high esteem. This shift in perspective holds the promise of heralding a future that is not only more prosperous, but also steeped in equity for one and all.

As I reflect on this collective spirit of giving and the aspiration to cultivate kindness and generosity in business, one of my heroines and role models is Khadija bint Khuwaylid, the wife of Prophet Mohammed (peace be upon him). Khadija was not only a successful businesswoman, but also a paragon of humility and charity. Her sagacious business acumen was complemented by her boundless generosity, especially towards the less fortunate.

Khadija's legacy serves as a beacon, guiding my resolve to ensure that kindness forms the bedrock of Gift Wellness. Her story fortifies my belief that it is possible for business to be a vehicle for compassion and positive change in the world, echoing the eternal values she so beautifully epitomised.

From selfie culture to social impact

The modern age of the 'selfie', with its emphasis on self-promotion, further amplifies the I agenda, and has an especially profound impact on young people. This fixation on physical appearance has culminated in a phenomenon known as 'beauty sickness', a term coined by Dr Renee Engeln, a psychologist and body image researcher at Northwestern University.[50]

Beauty sickness refers to the obsessive focus on one's appearance, leading to the diversion of cognitive, financial and emotional resources away from more meaningful pursuits. In her book *Beauty Sick*, Dr Engeln illuminates the harrowing effects of our society's infatuation with looks on the emotional and physical wellbeing of women and girls, as well as the ensuing financial toll and weakening of aspirations.[51] These repercussions encompass depression, eating disorders, cognitive impairments and squandered time and resources.

The evidence is compelling. The Office for National Statistics disclosed that between 2012 and 2020, there was a 94% surge in the number of women and girls who took their own lives, mirroring the grave toll of beauty sickness on our society.[52] In an age devoid of guiding principles, with technology advancing at a pace that outstrips human adaptability, chaos reigns supreme. This chaos is manifested in the tragic surge in suicides among young people, a stark and poignant testament to our moral decay.

As we venture further into the era of rapid technological advancement, particularly in AI, it is vital to scrutinise the nature and intentions underpinning online content. The trajectory that AI takes, whether as an instrument for good or otherwise, hinges on the information and data that we feed into the virtual world through our smartphones, social media and search engines. It is incumbent upon us to steer our focus away from the narcissistic culture of the selfie and towards the cultivation of a society that is altruistic, socially responsible and oriented towards positive change. Note to self: craft a campaign entitled 'From Selfie to Selfless'.

My aspiration was to establish a business that would stand as a paragon of what is achievable when financial objectives are harmoniously blended with social goals. A business that would foster positive change in the realms of women's rights, environmental sustainability and philanthropy, while also being financially viable. I was convinced that by placing social and environmental goals at the forefront, I could generate a business characterised by higher employee engagement and motivation, and that would resonate with socially conscious consumers, thus enhancing brand reputation and customer loyalty.

My zeal for women's empowerment guided me towards developing products that would be beneficial for women's bodies and provide comfort during menstruation. The vision was to instil a sense of benevolence in every purchase and to cater to the burgeoning demographic of socially conscious consumers. For the professionals and eco-conscious women who are inclined towards organic and fair-trade products, the ability to contribute to providing menstrual products to women in need offers them the gratification of knowing that their purchases are effecting positive change.

From its inception, the Gift Wellness social enterprise model has demonstrated its innate potential to be a hotbed for innovation, teeming with a plethora of creative solutions with social and environmental underpinnings. I have proven that by striking a balance between financial and social objectives, it is possible to formulate a business model that is not only sustainable, but also yields enduring impact.

The triumph of a social enterprise is contingent on a myriad of factors, including its business model, leadership and implementation strategies, but paramount among these are the intention, vision and ardour of its leader. A social enterprise transcends the confines of a conventional business; it is a movement, a conduit for positive change and a catalyst for transformation. I was unwavering in my resolve to create a business that would embody these principles and serve as a beacon of hope for generations to come.

The GIFT method

Venturing into a new project or business can be a daunting endeavour, particularly for those dipping their toes into the entrepreneurial pool for the first time. The GIFT method emerges as a lighthouse in these tumultuous waters, offering a set of guiding principles that I have honed over a decade of experience in rolling out projects, spearheading campaigns, establishing charities and nurturing businesses.

This method is instrumental in clarifying your core purpose, which in turn lays a robust foundation for your enterprise.

The GIFT method unfurls through a four-step process: gratitude, illustrate (your intention), focus and triple bottom line. Engaging with these steps prior to crafting your business plan yields a crucible for refining your intentions, dismantling emotional and confidence hurdles, and paving the path for the triumphant realisation of your aspirations.

Step 1: Gratitude

The maiden step in the GIFT method is gratitude, harnessing the past to fuel your future. This quintessential step helps you to triumph over the shackles of limiting beliefs that often spawn from a past tribulation – be it grief, turmoil, adversity or any emotional tumult that acts as a barricade in your path to success.

Gratitude transcends the superficial appreciation of obvious blessings like health and wealth; it delves deeper into acknowledging the crucible that hardships represent. By embracing the challenges and tribulations, and cherishing the wisdom they impart, you generate a propelling force that catapults you towards your aspirations.

Accepting that adversities can sculpt your character and metamorphose into a catalyst for positivity empowers you to harness this energy for profound transformation. Confronting adversities with the resolve to utilise them as fuel to achieve the remarkable unleashes your innate resilience and ingenuity. As Morihei Ueshiba explains in his book, *The Art of Peace,* 'Be grateful even for hardship, setbacks, and bad people. Dealing with such obstacles is an essential part of training in the Art of Peace.'[53] Therefore, let the wisdom distilled from tribulations be the kindling that intensifies your inner fire as you chase your dreams.

Here are a few ways to cultivate gratitude:

- For those who find solace in religion or meditation, **weave gratitude into your daily spiritual regimen through prayers or affirmations**. This practice channels your pent-up energy into a potent force, refocusing it on your vision and objectives.

- **Maintain a gratitude journal**, where you inscribe a minimum of three elements you are grateful for each day. Make it a point to include hardships or negative events, as acknowledging them is crucial.

- **Pen down your sentiments in a blog or article**, expressing your gratitude for the hardships and explaining why. You may choose to either publish it or keep it personal.

Initially, expressing gratitude for hardships may seem counterintuitive, but through conscious focus on the silver linings these events unfurl and by flexing your gratitude muscle as a daily ritual, you can initiate a paradigm shift. This practice aids in recalibrating your perspective towards optimism. Moreover, it serves as a repository of positive affirmations, especially on days when despondency creeps in.

Complementing gratitude for life's experiences, expressing appreciation towards the individuals who supported you through them is equally vital. This can manifest through a simple gesture such as a thank-you note or verbal acknowledgement. Not only does it positively impact the recipients, but it also bolsters your own mental health by fostering stronger bonds, enhancing self-esteem and alleviating stress and anxiety.

Tony Robbins' poignant words, 'When you are grateful, fear disappears and abundance appears',[54] emphasise the sheer power and necessity of practising gratitude. Through gratitude, even when the clouds of adversity loom, we possess the alchemy to transmute negativity into boundless positivity, sculpting the life we envision.

Step 2: Illustrate your intention

The second step in the GIFT method, illustrate your intention, is a pivotal juncture that breathes life into your grandiose vision. It necessitates unyielding clarity and precision in articulating your aims and purpose, giving form to a vision that emanates from the core of your being and is etched on to paper through the fluidity of your thoughts. The magnitude of this step is immeasurable, as it sets your deepest aspirations in motion and enriches your overall vision.

Upon crafting a vibrant illustration of your desired outcomes, you will find the task of homing in on the essential facets exponentially effortless. This acute focus allows you to orchestrate your energies with precision, driving you inexorably towards your destination.

Let me explain how to illustrate your intention.

Envision your future self

Embarking on this journey begins with projecting oneself into the tapestry of the future, precisely five years hence. Reflect deeply. Where do you yearn to be? What milestones do you envisage conquering? How does your idyllic life take shape?

Engaging in this act of envisioning your future self is a potent mechanism for outlining your aspirations and charting the course to fulfilment. As you undertake this mental odyssey, contemplate these guiding questions:

- Where do you envision yourself dwelling, working or voyaging?

- What kind of work will engage your spirit?

- How do you envisage your relationships evolving?

- What virtues do you seek to cultivate within yourself?

- What indelible impact do you aspire to etch upon the world?

These reflective queries serve to refine the silhouette of your envisioned future, intensifying your focus and fortifying your commitment.

Craft a mood board

Fabricating a mood board is an ingenious stratagem to give substance to your vision. This tactile canvas showcases your ambitions and aspirations in a tangible, evocative form.

Initiate it by defining your core purpose. What is the summit you are determined to scale? Upon solidifying your vision, proceed to collate images, quotations and any other visual elements that resonate with your aspirations. Let the images be ones that animate your soul and the words those that stir your heart.

Once your repository is amassed, proceed to arrange it on a physical or digital board. Your mood board is your personal sanctuary and may evolve as your vision takes sharper form. Place it in a location where it perpetually beckons your gaze, reminding and inspiring you daily.

Craft a narrative

If your inclinations lean towards auditory expression, weaving a narrative that encapsulates your vision could be your chosen medium. Detail a tapestry that describes your future self, five years hence. Paint a vivid verbal image of your surroundings, your endeavours, your companions and your emotional state. Such a narrative becomes your anchor, a written manifesto of your dreams. It's private and meant only for your eyes, serving as a fount of inspiration.

Construct a mind-map

If you're inclined towards analytical expression, creating a mind-map may resonate more deeply with you. A mind-map is an intricate diagram that weaves your thoughts into a visually cohesive tapestry. Central to it is your core idea, with tendrils extending outwards into subtopics, portraying the interplay between your thoughts. It's a dynamic and organic representation of your cognitive process, fostering critical evaluation of your vision.

Engage with your vision regularly

Regardless of the medium – be it mood board, narrative or mind-map – regular engagement is the key.

It's vital to immerse yourself in your vision daily, keeping the embers of motivation aflame. Regularly reflecting on your vision fortifies your resolve, focusing your energies on the task at hand.

In summary, illustrating your intention is the linchpin in giving life to your vision. This act of creation distils your vision into a tangible form. With a clear and focused vision, you illuminate your path, making it infinitely easier to tread the road leading to your dreams. As the renowned thinker Napoleon Hill once professed, 'Cherish your visions and your dreams as they are the children of your soul, the blueprints of your ultimate achievements.'[55]

Step 3: Focus

In the GIFT methodology, focus stands as the third crucial step, forming the nexus between your illustrated intentions and the tangible actions that manifest them, sharpening your sights and directing your energies. Focus is not merely the narrowing of attention; it is the forge wherein the molten metal of dreams is hammered into the unyielding steel of reality.

Focus is the magnifying glass that intensifies the sun's rays into a beam potent enough to ignite a flame. Through the lens of focus, your energies are harnessed, directed and channelled towards the relentless pursuit of your vision.

Here is my advice on how to forge focus.

Cultivate a focused mindset

First, recognise that the mind is often tossed around in a tumultuous sea of thoughts. It requires a lighthouse – a strong, unwavering beacon – to guide it through the tempests. Establishing this lighthouse is cultivating a focused mindset.

This begins with mindfulness – being aware of the ebb and flow of your thoughts and, with gentle resolution, steering them towards your goals. It is essential to avoid distractions and dispel negativities that cloud your mind. Instead, nourish your thoughts with positivity, resilience and an unyielding commitment to your vision.

Develop an action plan

While the mind is the architect, action is the mason that lays the bricks and mortar of your dreams. Formulating an action plan is critical in translating your mental blueprint into a physical structure.

Begin by dissecting your broader vision into smaller, more attainable milestones. For each milestone, delineate specific tasks and allocate timelines. By dividing your monumental dream into modular components, you render it not only more manageable, but infinitely more achievable.

Employing tools for focus

In this age of technology, an array of tools is at your disposal to augment your focus. From task management applications to digital journals, these tools serve as the scaffolding that supports the construction of your dreams. Employ them wisely to track progress, set reminders and ensure that your energies are always aligned with your tasks at hand.

Surround yourself with aligned energies

As the adage goes, 'You are the average of the five people you spend the most time with'. Surround yourself with individuals who not only resonate with your vision, but are themselves fonts of energy, passion and positivity. When you envelop yourself in an aura of aligned energies, you create a synergistic effect – where the collective sum is greater than the components.

Celebrate the small wins

The road to realising a grand vision is long and arduous. It is imperative to keep the flames of motivation alive by celebrating the small wins along the way. These celebrations need not be grandiose; sometimes, a moment of reflection and gratitude is enough to replenish your energies.

In summation, focus is the catalyst that accelerates the reaction between your dreams and actions. It is the alchemy that transmutes the ethereal into the tangible. With a focused mindset, a well-crafted action plan, the wise utilisation of tools, surrounded by a band of passionate allies and raising celebratory toasts at every milestone, you ensure your vision is not a mere possibility – it becomes an impending reality. As Alexander Graham Bell once stated, 'Concentrate all your thoughts upon the work at hand. The sun's rays do not burn until brought to a focus.'[56]

Step 4: Triple bottom line

The crowning gem of the GIFT methodology is the triple bottom line, a concept that represents the culmination of your intentions, focus and actions into a sustainable and harmonious entity. It is the realisation that true success is not just the accumulation of wealth, but the enrichment of our communities and the stewardship of our planet.

The triple bottom line calls for an intricate balance between three key pillars: people, planet and profit. It is a testament that business and benevolence are not only compatible, but are indeed the yin and yang of enduring success.

Here, we look at the three pillars, and the implementation and rewards of the triple bottom line.

People: Kindness as a keystone

The first element of the triple bottom line is people. This means recognising the intrinsic value of human beings and the communities that you serve. Kindness must be the keystone upon which your venture is constructed.

This entails not only the fair and respectful treatment of employees, but also the nurturing of positive relationships with customers, partners and the community. It's about creating a culture that values diversity, inclusion and the betterment of society.

Planet: Stewardship for sustainability

The second pillar, planet, reflects the imperative role of environmental stewardship. It is an acknowledgement that our planet's resources are not inexhaustible and that it is incumbent upon us to utilise them judiciously.

This involves minimising your ecological footprint through sustainable practices such as reducing waste, conserving energy, and integrating eco-friendly materials and technologies. By adopting environmentally sustainable practices, you are not just safeguarding the planet for future generations, but also building a brand that resonates with the increasingly eco-conscious consumer.

Profit: Ethical earnings and enduring value

The final pillar, profit, represents the financial aspect of the venture. However, within the ambit of the triple bottom line, it is profit earned ethically and responsibly. It is profit used not just for enrichment, but for empowerment – of your venture, your community and your environment. This involves creating a sustainable business model that can withstand the test of time and continuously add value to society.

Implementing the triple bottom line

One of the most potent ways to concretise the triple bottom line is through the incorporation of giving back into your business model. By allocating a portion of your profits to charitable causes or engaging in community projects, you demonstrate that your venture is not just a business, but a movement. This, in turn, fosters an emotional bond with your customers and community, who see themselves not just as consumers, but as partners in a large, noble cause.

Welcoming alignment and continuous improvement

With the triple bottom line at the helm, your venture will naturally attract like-minded individuals, be they investors, partners, employees or customers. This fortuitous alignment creates a virtuous cycle of positivity, trust and mutual enrichment. However, it is essential to maintain a culture of continuous improvement, to listen to feedback and to evolve in response to the changing needs of society and the environment.

In summation, the triple bottom line is the grand finale of the GIFT methodology. It is where your gratitude, your illustrated vision and your focused actions converge into a symphony of sustainability, responsibility and kindness. It is a manifestation of the belief that your business is not an island, but a part of a larger ecosystem – one that it must nourish as much as it draws nourishment. In embracing the triple bottom line, you do not just build a venture; you sow the seeds of a legacy.

Conclusion

As I reflect on the extraordinary journey of the past fifteen years, I am in awe of the distances I've traversed and the peaks I've scaled. The loss of Halimah was a tragedy that moulded me. I was shaped by the excruciating pain and raw vulnerability it elicited. Yet, paradoxically, it acted as a chrysalis, within which I discovered my true essence. This harrowing experience unmasked my authentic self, unearthing a fearlessness and resilience I didn't know I possessed. It freed me from the chains of societal expectations, launching me on to a path of self-empowerment and individuality, and set the stage for the cause-driven entrepreneurial journey that lay ahead.

Halimah's departure marked a transformational pivot in my life, unshackling me from the fear and self-doubt that had stifled my voice, and kindling a resolute commitment to authenticity. This confidence propelled me to channel my grief into purpose, and in the wake of profound loss, The Halimah Trust and Gift Wellness were born. Little did I know, the journey ahead would be punctuated by an evolving technological landscape, the birth of social media and the rapid advancement of digital platforms. Despite the challenges, my resilience and determination enabled me to craft a successful business model centred around a cause that ignited my passion.

This path was not always illuminated, at times mirroring the chaos of the Wild West. I encountered hurdles and made mistakes, but every one was an opportunity, a hidden treasure waiting to be unearthed; each misstep was a lesson learned, a stepping stone leading me to greater heights.

Perhaps my greatest accomplishment is the unyielding perseverance that has seen me through every storm. The potency of my vision served as an unwavering beacon, guiding me even when I was faced with the potential loss of all my retailers during the pandemic, dismissive reactions towards menstrual products and pressures from larger brands. I stood my ground, confident in the knowledge that I had been positioned on this path for a greater purpose.

This belief manifested in the positive impact the Halimah School of Excellence and College in Pakistan, the women in refugee camps and countless customers of my products have experienced. Their gratitude fuels my fervour to continually strive for more.

As Gift Wellness grows, I stand on the cusp of boundless possibilities, my heart aflutter with excitement for the blossoming generation of socially conscious change makers. They are the torchbearers, intuitively attuned to the cries of our ailing planet and the plight of fellow humans. In concert with them, Gift Wellness steadfastly marches on, aspiring to be more than a business; it's a lighthouse guiding those who, akin to me, have sculpted their tribulations into a great purpose.

Throughout these pages, I've endeavoured to offer you a glimpse into the bounty of gifts my destiny has graciously lavished upon me: my darling daughter, our shared charity, the solace in my faith and the tapestry that is Gift Wellness, but what is the essence, the quintessence, that *The Gift* as a title seeks to distil? It is the epiphany that the supreme gift is the test – the crucible itself.

The anguish and soul-searching that enveloped me in the wake of losing my beloved Halimah metamorphosed into the alchemy that guided me to my life's calling. Solaced by the conviction that our parting is but an interlude, how could I not embrace each dawn with fervour to weave a tapestry of love and legacy in her name – a tapestry that will whisper her song to the winds long after I am reunited with her? May my narrative embolden you to unearth your own purpose, to transmute your challenges into stepping stones that lead you to realms uncharted.

As we arrive at the shores of this book's final pages, my soul is awash with gratitude, my spirit buoyed by the conviction that our rendezvous was not the whimsy of chance, but the symphony of destiny. I stand before you, humbled to my core, profoundly grateful for the serenade of your presence as our energies dance in harmony through the words and phrases. I have bared my soul, intertwining my hopes, vulnerabilities and aspirations with yours, and in doing so, I have birthed a bond with you that defies the finite nature of this book.

Our union, I fervently believe, was orchestrated by the Divine, each note in perfect harmony for a purpose – to be a balm, a spark, a whisper of joy, a lighthouse in the tempest. Our paths, interwoven in the boundless tapestry of existence, were fated to cross. Thank you for traversing this odyssey with me, for granting me the honour of a sojourn in your journey.

As the final words bid adieu, let us part with this. Know that your essence is immeasurable, your ripples through the cosmos carry the whispers of ages, and within the wondrous mosaic of existence, your thread weaves magic, grace and infinite possibility.

Join Gift Wellness:
Five Pathways To Impact

Inviting change into our lives is a transformative act of courage, grace and potential. Each of us has the power to effect change, to shape lives and to weave narratives of hope, resilience and empowerment.

Now I extend a heartfelt invitation to you, inviting you to join me on this journey towards impact. Your engagement helps Gift Wellness in eradicating period poverty, promoting workplace inclusivity and championing women's health.

Here are five ways in which you can actively be a part of this change.

Empower through purchase

The driving force behind my brand's ability to foster change is the sales of Gift products. By choosing my products – especially the Gift pads, featuring anion tourmaline technology to actively support menstrual health – you are making an investment not only in your wellbeing, but also in the sustainability of our planet and in providing crucial support to women in crisis.

Call to action: embrace this cause by using the discount code TryGift for 50% off your first purchase. Consider setting up a subscription for ongoing savings, free doorstep delivery and access to exclusive offers. Make the change that makes a difference. Available at https://giftwellness.co.uk.

Advocate for accessible menstrual products

Gift Wellness is championing employers to supply free menstrual products in their washrooms, a small yet powerful initiative fostering trust and respect in the workplace. This cost-effective solution holds the potential to revolutionise workplaces for the betterment of future generations.

Call to action: are you an employer ready to make this commitment? Sign up for Gift's service here: https://giftwellness.co.uk/collections/workplaces.

Be a catalyst for workplace transformation

Gift Wellness's FFW consultancy, with the aid of VR, fosters empathy and combats stigmas, especially in male-dominated sectors. I envision a workplace that understands and respects women's physiological needs and fosters a supportive environment.

Call to action: are you an employer ready to transform your workplace? Schedule a free discovery consultation at www.femalefriendlyworkplaces.com.

Join the fight against period poverty

Gift Wellness's Period Angels app is a significant stride towards creating a self-sustaining ecosystem aimed at eradicating period poverty, starting from every community in Britain and eventually reaching every corner of the world. This initiative enables Gift Wellness to focus its efforts on complex issues such as the plight of women in refugee camps and economically challenged regions.

Call to action: do you run a charity or food bank, or are you a volunteer eager to participate in this initiative? Download the Period Angels app today, available on iOS and Android, and make a donation to support this work at www.periodpoverty.uk.

Champion the education of girls in Pakistan

The Halimah School and College in Wazirabad, Pakistan, stand as a beacon of hope, promising quality education for over 1,000 orphaned and needy girls. By supporting their growth and education, you can catalyse their transformation into empowered women, ready to effect positive change in their own lives and communities. Your contribution will ensure the continued growth of this vital institution, offering girls a fighting chance at a future defined by knowledge, independence and opportunities.

Call to action: ready to become a champion for girls' education? Learn more and offer your support at www.halimahtrust.org.uk. Every contribution makes a significant difference.

References

1   C Barks and J Moyne (translators), *The Essential Rumi* (HarperCollins, 1995)
2   ZR Ahmed (Lyricist) and F Ahmed (Performer), 'One Day' [Song] (2008), www.youtube.com/watch?v=CiimmOdC W0A&list=RDCiimmOdCW0A&start_radio=1, accessed August 2023
3   C Barks and J Moyne (translators), *The Essential Rumi* (HarperCollins, 1995)
4   C Tingle and S Vora, 'Break the barriers: Girls' experiences of menstruation in the UK' (Plan International UK, 2017), https://plan-uk.org/file/plan-uk-break-the-barriers-report-032018pdf/download?token=Fs-HYP3v, accessed July 2023
5   T Burke, 'The #metoo Movement' (no date), https://metoomvmt.org, accessed April 2021
6   F Taylor, 'In her shoes' (Centrepoint, 2022), https://centrepoint.org.uk/media/5626/in-her-shoes-young-womens-research.pdf, accessed December 2022
7   C Tingle and S Vora, 'Break the barriers: Girls' experiences of menstruation in the UK' (Plan International UK, 2017), https://plan-uk.org/file/plan-uk-break-the-barriers-report-032018pdf/download?token=Fs-HYP3v, accessed July 2023

8 United Nations, 'A record 100 million people forcibly displaced worldwide', *UN News* (2022), https://news.un.org/en/story/2022/05/1118772, accessed June 2022

9 CHEM Trust, 'The harmful chemicals that might be present in your menstrual products' (Women's Environmental Network, 24 November 2020), www.wen.org.uk/2020/11/24/the-harmful-chemicals-that-might-be-present-in-your-menstrual-products, accessed June 2021

10 A Chisholm, 'Toxic chemicals in your tampons', *Verywell Health* (2022), www.verywellhealth.com/toxic-chemicals-in-your-tampons-2721810, accessed August 2023

11 University of La Plata, '85% of tampons, pads and other feminine care products contaminated with Monsanto's cancer-causing, endocrine-disrupting glyphosate', *Women of Green* (15 February 2017), https://womenofgreen.com/2017/02/15/85-of-tampons-pads-and-other-feminine-care-products-contaminated-with-monsantos-cancer-causing-endocrine-disrupting-glyphosate, accessed July 2023

12 M Bajirova, 'Miraculous effects of negative ions on urogenital infections', *Obstetrics and Gynecology International Journal*, 9/1 (2018), https://doi.org/10.15406/ogij.2018.09.00297, accessed 2 October 2023; F Vatansever and MR Hamblin, 'Far infrared radiation (FIR): Its biological effects and medical applications/*Ferne Infrarotstrahlung: Biologische Effekte und medizinische Anwendungen*', *Photonics and Lasers in Medicine*, 1/4 (2012), 255–266, https://doi.org/10.1515/plm-2012-0034, accessed October 2023

13 L Bland, 'What is tourmaline and why do we use it in our pads?' (Gift Wellness, no date), https://giftwellness.co.uk/blogs/news/what-is-tourmaline-and-why-do-we-use-it-in-our-pads, accessed July 2023

14 Z Hu and C Sun, 'A study on preparation and utilization of tourmaline from tailings of an iron-ore processing plant', *Procedia Environmental Sciences*, 31 (2016), 153–161, www.researchgate.net/publication/301745298_An_Study_on_Preparation_and_Utilization_of_Tourmaline_from_Tailings_of_an_Iron-ore_Processing_Plant, accessed October 2023

15 Ibid

16 Gift Wellness, customer reviews (YouTube, 2019), www.youtube.com/watch?v=3ZTx1izI18Y, accessed July 2023

17 J Singha Ray, 'Child labor, children, mining' (The Borgen Project, no date), https://borgenproject.org/tag/child-miners-in-developing-countries, accessed February 2023

18 C Barks and J Moyne (translators), *The Essential Rumi* (HarperCollins, 1995)

19 National Institute for Health and Care Excellence, 'Endometriosis: How common is it?' (2020), https://cks.nice.org.uk/topics/endometriosis/background-information/prevalence, accessed August 2023

20 CM Matthews, 'Nurturing *your* divine feminine', *Proceedings of the Baylor University Medical Center*, 24/3 (2011), 248, www.ncbi.nlm.nih.gov/pmc/articles/PMC3124912, accessed March 2023

21 H Harris, 'Endometriosis linked to childhood abuse' (Fred Hutchinson Cancer Research Center, 2018), www.fredhutch.org/en/news/center-news/2018/07/endometriosis-linked-to-childhood-abuse.html, accessed February 2023

22 F Facchin, G Barbara, E Saita, P Mosconi, A Roberto, L Fedele and P Vercellini, 'Impact of endometriosis on quality of life and mental health: Pelvic pain makes the difference', *Journal of Psychosomatic Obstetrics & Gynecology*, 36/4 (2015), 135–141

23 M Armour, A Middleton, S Lim, J Sinclair, D Varjabedian and CA Smith, 'Dietary practices of women with endometriosis: A cross-sectional survey', *The Journal of Alternative and Complementary Medicine*, 27/9 (2021), 771–777, https://doi.org/10.1089/acm.2021.0068, accessed August 2023

24 R Veenhoven, 'Healthy happiness: Effects of happiness on physical health and the consequences for preventive health care', *Journal of Happiness Studies*, 9/3 (2008), 449–469

25 JM Ussher, 'Managing the monstrous feminine: Regulating the reproductive body', *Social Science & Medicine*, 63/9 (2006), 2378–2387

26 KFS Petrelluzzi, MC Garcia, CA Petta, DM Grassi-Kassisse and RC Spadari-Bratfisch, 'Salivary cortisol concentrations, stress and quality of life in women with endometriosis and chronic pelvic pain', *Stress: The International Journal on the Biology of Stress*, 11/5 (2008), 390–397

27 M Armour, J Sinclair, KJ Chalmers and CA Smith, 'Self-management strategies amongst Australian women with endometriosis: A national online survey', *BMC*

Complementary and Alternative Medicine, 19/17 (2019), https://doi.org/10.1186/s12906-019-2431-x, accessed August 2023

28 C Barks and J Moyne (translators), *The Essential Rumi* (HarperCollins, 1995)

29 T Burke, 'The #metoo Movement' (no date), https://metoomvmt.org; C Tingle and S Vora, 'Break the barriers: Girls' experiences of menstruation in the UK' (Plan International UK, 2018), https://plan-uk.org/file/plan-uk-break-the-barriers-report-032018pdf/download?token=Fs-HYP3v, accessed July 2023

30 RW Connell and JW Messerschmidt, 'Hegemonic masculinity: Rethinking the concept', *Gender and Society*, 19/6 (2005), 829–859, www.jstor.org/stable/27640853, accessed March 2023

31 R Jewkes et al, 'Hegemonic masculinity: Combining theory and practice in gender interventions', *Culture, Health & Sexuality*, 17/2 (2015), 112–127, www.tandfonline.com/doi/full/10.1080/13691058.2015.1085094, accessed March 2023

32 CM Matthews, 'Nurturing *your* divine feminine', *Proceedings of the Baylor University Medical Center*, 24/3 (2011), 248, www.ncbi.nlm.nih.gov/pmc/articles/PMC3124912, accessed March 2023

33 K Nicholson, 'Iceland boss points out UK has more food banks than McDonald's branches', *Huffington Post* (24 September 2021), www.huffingtonpost.co.uk/entry/mcdonalds-food-banks-iceland-question-time_uk_614d91b7e4b001641192a1fe, accessed December 2022

34 Z Ahmed, 'A mother's gift to humanity – Period justice' (TEDx, 2021), https://youtu.be/viJNOUy3hU8, accessed July 2023

35 M Armstrong, 'It will take another 136 years to close the global gender gap' (World Economic Forum, 12 April 2021), www.weforum.org/agenda/2021/04/136-years-is-the-estimated-journey-time-to-gender-equality, accessed February 2023

36 C Barks and J Moyne (translators), *The Essential Rumi* (HarperCollins, 1995)

37 Oceana, 'Tackling the plastics crisis at the source' (no date), https://usa.oceana.org/our-campaigns/plastic, accessed November 2022

38 A Roddick, *Business as Unusual: The journey of Anita Roddick and the Body Shop* (HarperCollins, 2000)

39 C Parker, 'Brits recycle in the kitchen but not in the bathroom, plus other recycling truths', *Huffington Post* (27 September 2018), www.huffingtonpost.co.uk/entry/brits-recycle-in-kitchen-but-not-in-the-bathroom-plus-other-home-truths_uk_5bab9d68e4b082030e772a05, accessed March 2023

40 C Tingle and S Vora, 'Break the barriers: Girls' experiences of menstruation in the UK', Plan International UK (2018), https://plan-uk.org/file/plan-uk-break-the-barriers-report-032018pdf/download?token=Fs-HYP3v, accessed July 2023

41 McKinsey & Company and Lean In, *Women in the Workplace 2022* (2022), www.mckinsey.com/featured-insights/diversity-and-inclusion/women-in-the-workplace, accessed August 2023; P Gaudiano, 'Women's equality in the workplace requires greater inclusion', *Forbes* (8 March 2022), www.forbes.com/sites/paologaudiano/2022/03/08/womens-equality-in-the-workplace-requires-greater-inclusion, accessed August 2023; C Ammerman and B Groysberg, 'How to close the gender gap: You have to be systematic', *Harvard Business Review* (May–June 2021), https://hbr.org/2021/05/how-to-close-the-gender-gap, accessed August 2023

42 https://spark-media.co.uk

43 PwC, 'Seeing is believing' (2020), www.pwc.com/seeingisbelieving, accessed February 2022

44 Z Ahmed, 'A mother's gift to humanity – Period justice' (TEDx, 2021), https://youtu.be/viJNOUy3hU8, accessed July 2023

45 D Priestley, *Key Person of Influence: The five-step method to become one of the most highly valued and highly paid people in your industry* (Rethink Press, 2014)

46 OpenAI, ChatGPT (no date), https://openai.com, accessed December 2022

47 C Barks and J Moyne (translators), *The Essential Rumi* (HarperCollins, 1995)

48 K Miller, 'The triple bottom line: What it is & why it's important' (Harvard Business School, 8 December 2020), https://online.hbs.edu/blog/post/what-is-the-triple-bottom-line, accessed February 2023

49 J Sacks, *Morality: Restoring the common good in divided times* (Hodder & Stoughton, 2020)

50 R Engeln (personal website), Dr Renee Engeln's Body and Media Lab (Northwestern University), http://bodyandmedia.com, accessed March 2023

51 R Engeln, *Beauty Sick: How the cultural obsession with appearance hurts girls and women* (Harper, 2018)

52 United Nations, 'Figures at a glance' report, *UN News* (June 2023), www.unhcr.org/about-unhcr/who-we-are/figures-glance, accessed June 2023; M Bulman, 'Suicides among teenage girls and young women have almost doubled in seven years, figures show', *The Independent* (1 September 2020), www.independent.co.uk/news/uk/home-news/suicides-teenage-girls-young-women-rise-figures-a9698296.html, accessed November 2023

53 M Ueshiba, *The Art of Peace: Teachings of the founder of Aikido Pocket Classic* (Shambhala Publications, 1992)

54 T Robbins, *Unlimited Power: The new science of personal achievement* (Simon & Schuster UK, 2001)

55 N Hill, *Think and Grow Rich* (Vermilion, 2004)

56 OS Marden, Chapter 2, interview with Bell, in: *How They Succeeded: Life stories of successful men told by themselves* (Lothrop, Lee and Shepard, 1901)

Acknowledgements

My soul swells with gratitude as I reflect on the constellation of benevolent spirits that have guided me through the tempestuous odyssey of my life. In the crucible of losing a child, the very fabric of one's being is tested. My solace was the sanctuary of love and compassion cradled within the embrace of my family. With hearts heavy, often fumbling for words, they provided a steadfast presence, which was the beacon that guided me through the fog.

To my parents, siblings and cherished in-laws, many of whom have graced the pages of this book, thank you for being the unwavering pillars that held me aloft. A special embrace to my sister-in-law Nahida, whose boundless love cascaded like a guardian angel's wings upon my children, Ash and me.

Friends and colleagues have adorned my path with kindness and camaraderie; to you, I extend a heartfelt embrace. Above all, my gratitude spirals upwards to Allah, my creator, who deemed me worthy to be the bearer of this sacred chalice of trials. As my life unravels, in whispered winds and serendipitous moments, I am reminded that each thread has purpose, leading to an ordained symphony. The sanctuary of my prayer is my anchor. The wise words of Imam Al-Shafi'i, 'My heart is at ease knowing that what was meant for me will never miss me, and that what misses me was never meant for me', whisper to my soul, guiding me to dance to the rhythm of destiny.

To my son Faizaan, whose tender years were painted with the grace and wisdom of sages; you emerged from the crucible a phoenix, your wings sheltering Ash and me. Your wisdom is the compass that has guided us through the tumultuous seas, your gentle spirit a reminder of the tapestry woven by the Divine. Your metamorphosis into a devoted husband, doting father and entrepreneur fills me with pride; you are the lullaby in my heart, the coolness of my eyes, my dearest Faizaan.

Dr Sam Collins, CEO and founder of Aspire, materialised as an architect of transformation within my growth. Her indomitable spirit and vision as a beacon for women's leadership redefined my own route, igniting my journey towards empowerment. Dr Collins, thank you for illuminating my path; you have unlocked the tapestry of my feminine strength that had lain reticent beneath layers of patriarchy and tradition.

As the confluence of technology and marketing evolved, Daniel Priestley's *Key Person of Influence* programme guided me into uncharted waters. His insights into the heart of a brand, its story and the mountain of value that is one's journey were revelations. Under his tutelage, Gift Wellness bloomed and adapted, a nimble vessel amid changing tides. My gratitude to Daniel and the kinship within the Dent Global family is boundless; you have been the wind in my sails.

To the mentors, kindred spirits and guides who have woven magic into my journey, my heart sings your praises.

To my Ash, my anchor and my sanctuary; in you, I find the reflection of my soul. Our tapestry is one of symbiosis, a dance of spirits that nurtures, shields and emboldens. The Quran's verse, 'They (women) are garments for you (men) and you are garments for them' [2:187], resonates with the essence of our union. Your love is the mantle that envelops us in grace through the symphony of our journey.

To all who have painted strokes of love, wisdom and generosity upon the canvas of my life, my soul bows in gratitude. May your kindness be woven into the fabric of eternity.

The Author

Dr Zareen Roohi Ahmed, a multi-faceted entrepreneur and expert, has been a beacon of innovation, leadership and change for over twenty-five years. Holding a PhD in multiculturalism, specialising in women's rights, her academic foundation is just the tip of the iceberg. From spearheading urban regeneration initiatives to her esteemed role as the CEO of the British Muslim Forum, representing Britain on foreign office delegations, her experience speaks volumes about her dynamism.

More than a seasoned professional, Zareen's heart beats for philanthropy. As the Chair of The Halimah

Trust, she transformed personal grief into global good, founding the charity in honour of her daughter. Her vision has always been vast, as evidenced by her pioneering work as the founder and CEO of Gift Wellness. This trailblazing social enterprise boasts an award-winning range of natural toiletries that have not only received accolades but catalysed a movement against period poverty. Distributing millions of menstrual products at home and abroad to homeless women, refugees, food banks and hospitals, Zareen's efforts are truly transformative. Amplifying this endeavour, she introduced the Gift Wellness Foundation and its innovative app, Period Angels, which serves as a community-led remedy for period poverty.

Always pushing boundaries, Zareen's most recent undertaking is an innovative consultancy targeting the underlying issues of discrimination against women in professional settings. By intertwining reproductive rights training with the magic of VR technology, this programme offers a novel perspective on the experiences of women, making workplaces more inclusive and empathetic.

Beyond her ground-breaking ventures, Zareen is a sought-after keynote speaker and podcast guest, enlightening audiences on topics such as social impact, women in the workplace and sustainability. As a lecturer in social entrepreneurship and a business coach, her insights have guided budding change-makers. Her published works further solidify her standing as a luminary in her field.

THE AUTHOR

🌐 www.giftwellness.co.uk

🌐 www.halimahtrust.org.uk

🌐 www.zareenroohi.com

in www.linkedin.com/in/
dr-zareen-roohi-ahmed-phd-3b51b219

f @zareen.r.ahmed

f @giftwellnessuk

✕ @GiftWellnessLtd

▶ www.youtube.com/channel/
UCsDroqHHnTnZyTAQU16e0cA